Curación
con el nopal

Curación
con el nopal

Editorial Época, S.A. de C.V.

Emperadores 185

Col. Portales

C.P. 03300 México, D. F.

Curación con el nopal
Rubén Villacis Villalba

© Derechos reservados 2009
© Editorial Época, S.A. de C.V.
Emperadores No. 185
C.P. 03300 — México, D.F.
E-mail: edesa2004@prodigy.net.mx
Tels: 56049046
56049072

ISBN: 970-627-751-X
978-970-627-751-0

Impreso en México — *Printed in Mexico*

Introducción

El aprovechamiento de las propiedades curativas de las plantas es una práctica milenaria que nunca ha dejado de existir.

El caso del nopal en México tiene un especial significado por el papel simbólico del asentamiento de los aztecas en el lago de Texcoco, dando lugar a su imperio, Tenochtitlan (*te*, piedra y *nochtli*, nopal). Los aztecas le daban muchos usos medicinales: para las fiebres bebían el jugo; la pulpa curaba la diarrea; el mucílago o baba del nopal lo utilizaron para curar labios partidos; las espinas, para la limpieza de infecciones; la fruta era utilizada para el exceso de bilis; empleaban las pencas del nopal como apósito caliente para aliviar inflamaciones; y la raíz para el tratamiento de hernia, hígado irritado, úlceras estomacales y erisipela.

El nopal es una planta silvestre que sobrevive en regiones desérticas y frías. No requiere de mucha agua para su cultivo, sus hojas (pencas) miden aproximadamente treinta centímetros de diámetro.

En cuanto a utilizarla para beneficios de salud, se recomienda que la tomen personas que padecen de diabetes, ya que incrementa los niveles y la sensibilidad a la insulina logrando que se regule el nivel de azúcar en la sangre. También las personas que poseen colesterol elevado, ya que ayuda a eliminarlo, evitando que se absorba gran parte de éste y así no se acumula en venas y arterias. Los aminoácidos y la fibra contenida en el nopal previenen que el exceso de azúcar en la sangre se convierta en grasa, mientras que actúa metabolizando la grasa y los ácidos grasos reduciendo así el colesterol.

En cuanto a su forma de consumirse es variada, ya que puede ingerirse en dulces, bebidas, ensaladas, sopas y guisos.

El nopal es una planta llena de espinas, pero que al igual que el rosal, nos ofrece hermosura a través de sus grandes beneficios alimenticios y medicinales; su flor, la tuna, es fruto rico en vitaminas y además es diurético.

El nopal, planta que identifica a nuestro país y que está estampado en el escudo nacional, también figura en la leyenda de la llegada de los aztecas a lo que hoy es México.

El nopal

El nopal es una planta silvestre que sobrevive en regiones desérticas y frías. No requiere de mucha agua para su cultivo, por lo que es una buena fuente de ingresos para muchos agricultores que no cuentan con los recursos necesarios y viven en zonas áridas o semiáridas. Se dice que tiene un papel ecológico importante, ya que detiene la degradación del suelo deforestado, o sea, convierte tierras improductivas en productivas. Existen cerca de mil seiscientas especies de la familia de las cactáceas, de la cual proviene el nopal. Tiene frutos, los cuales son comestibles y se conocen con el nombre de tunas. En México la ingesta anual *per cápita* de nopal es de 6.4 kilos.

El nopal pertenece al género Opuntia, de la familia de las cactáceas (*Cactaceae*). Algunas especies son: *Opuntia sp*; Nopal de tuna camuesa (*Opuntia robusta*); nopal cardón (*O. streptacantha*); tuna colorada (*O. stenopetala*); chaveña (*O. Chavena*); de castilla o higo chumbo (*O. ficus indica*); duraznilla (*O.leucotricha*); nopal de la cochinilla (*Nopalea cochenillifera*); tapona (*O. tapona*); xoconoscle o túna huell (*O. imbricata*).

Descripción de la planta

Es un arbusto de unos cinco metros de altura. Habita en clima seco, semiseco y templado. Su crecimiento óptimo se da en zonas áridas y semiáridas, aunque puede desarrollarse en cualquier clima.

Se caracteriza por los tallos planos o pencas en forma de paleta, cubiertos de pequeños agrupamientos de pelos rígidos llamados gloquidios y por lo general, también de espinas. Son verdes y los más jóvenes presentan hojas con forma de escama. Los ejemplares viejos pierden las palas inferiores y aparece entonces un tallo leñoso que da a la planta aspecto de árbol. Las flores amarillas y rojas nacen en los bordes de las palas, dan lugar a un fruto verrugoso piriforme llamado tuna o higo chumbo (en España), comestible, de pulpa carnosa y dulce. Se usa también como planta ornamental.

Las pencas de nopal son un alimento delicioso cuando se consumen casi en crudo, ligeramente asadas. También sirven como forraje para el ganado.

Contienen proteínas y minerales como calcio y potasio; son ligeramente laxantes; contribuyen a disminuir los niveles de colesterol y de glucosa y facilitan la eliminación de parásitos.

El fruto es conocido bajo el nombre de tuna, que es una baya ovoidea, rojiza, comestible y con diminutas semillas.

¿Cómo es su reproducción?

Su reproducción es muy sencilla, ya que cuando caen las pencas del nopal, basta que queden poco enterradas para que nazcan nuevas pencas y así se van reproduciendo. A veces se hace por semillas. También se planta la rama espinosa al ras del suelo, después de haberla dejado secar por unos días.

El tipo de ecosistema donde habita generalmente es en la estepa y en el desierto, ya que son zonas de poca lluvia en las que a veces predominan las condiciones desérticas, aunque las estepas son menos áridas que los desiertos y muestran un paisaje de grandes planicies, con vegetación de escasa altura.

En México el nopal se encuentra distribuido en casi todo el país, principalmente en las regiones áridas y semiáridas, de donde se le lleva a los grandes centros de consumo, es decir, las ciudades.

¿Cómo se adapta al ambiente?

El medio físico donde habita el nopal se caracteriza por tener veranos calurosos e inviernos muy fríos. Tiene dos períodos de lluvias escasas. La baja cantidad de lluvia y humedad crea un ambiente difícil para la existencia de plantas y animales.

El nopal es una planta que suele tener tallos hinchados y carnosos adaptados para la acumulación de agua; sus raíces son extensas y superficiales, sus hojas están reducidas a espinas, de tal manera que tienen agua almacenada que utilizan cuando no llueve. El nopal se caracteriza por su capacidad para soportar extensos períodos de sequía, ya que sus raíces extensas y superficiales le permiten la rápida absorción de humedad en cuanto ésta se presenta, aún cuando se trate de lluvias ligeras.

Desarrolla raíces muy largas para tomar agua del subsuelo.

El nopal aún no está en peligro de extinción, pero puede estarlo en cualquier momento, ya que algunos países se empiezan a interesar en él, porque se ha descubierto la gran cantidad de propiedades que de él se pueden aprovechar. Por ejemplo, de su fruto se pueden obtener vitaminas y propiedades astringentes y antisépticas; se utiliza para producir cierto tipo de miel, vino, alcohol y confituras como el queso de tuna. Por su parte, las pencas de nopal son un alimento delicioso; también sirven como forraje para el ganado; además son medicinales.

El nopal en verdura es un producto que ha ocupado un lugar importante en la dieta del mexicano, ya sea por tradición o por lo económico. En los últimos años se ha diversificado su uso y es ampliamente aceptado por la población en general. Como consecuencia, su cultivo se ha extendido en todas las regiones del país y su empleo ya no se limita sólo a los antiguos usos esenciales.

Al nopal también lo usan como barrera de protección, por sus afiladas espinas.

En los últimos años ha resurgido el interés por el nopal como fuente alimenticia y de salud, de manera que se ha incrementado su consumo no sólo en su estado fresco, sino también deshidratado como un complemento indicado en la medicina naturista.

Por lo anterior, se debe tener cuidado de no agotar este recurso natural, que antes era menospreciado y ahora se deben de tomar medidas necesarias para seguirlo cultivando en mayores proporciones y con mejores técnicas para su investigación y explotación.

Propiedades del nopal

Propiedades alimenticias

El nopal se usa como forraje, pero igualmente se comercializan las pencas tiernas como verdura; éstas se pueden preparar en escabeche, se cocinan en caldos y sopas, en ensaladas o en guisados; en platos fuertes, como antojitos; en salsas, bebidas, postres, mermeladas y un sinfín de usos alimenticios que se le puede dar a esta planta tan rica en propiedades.

Recientemente ha sido muy popular el consumo de nopales licuados con alguna fruta como medida para bajar de peso o para personas que padecen ciertas enfermedades. El único problema de esto es que a muchas personas les es un poco desagradable el mucílago o baba, ya que al hacer el licuado se queda ahí.

El polvo de nopal o nopal deshidratado, ha venido a ofrecer una solución para este inconveniente. Para evitar la baba del nopal se congela o se cuela, se recomienda también ajo, bicarbonato, cáscara de tomate, hoja de maíz, jugo de limón, ceniza o piedra volcánica en el agua.

Propiedades nutricionales

En lo que respecta al valor nutricional del nopal, se puede decir que en una taza de nopales crudos (86 gramos aproximadamente) hay 2.9 gramos de hidratos de carbono, 1.1 gramos de proteína y solamente 14 kilocalorías. Pero su principal atractivo es que contiene una gran cantidad de fibra dietética (soluble e insoluble): 2 gramos de fibra en una taza. Existe una relación 30:70 de fibra soluble a insoluble. La fibra insoluble puede prevenir y aliviar el estreñimiento y las hemorroides, al mismo tiempo que previene la aparición de cáncer de colon. La fibra soluble se ha usado en muchos padecimientos, porque su presencia en el tubo digestivo retarda la absorción de nutrimentos y hace que estos no pasen a la sangre rápidamente. También son una buena fuente de calcio, ya que en 100 gramos de nopales, hay aproximadamente 80 miligramos de calcio.

Propiedades medicinales

Se han demostrado en varios estudios, principalmente realizados en México, las cualidades terapéuticas que tiene el nopal. Se les llama "propiedades medicinales" ya que ayudan a controlar la enfermedad con mayor facilidad, sin que esto signifique que sea el responsable de la curación total.

Desde tiempos prehispánicos se utiliza en la medicina popular, y varias de sus propiedades curativas han sido confirmadas por investigaciones llevadas a cabo recientemente. En el Códice de la Cruz-Badiano se observa un nopal acompañado de un texto en el cual se afirma que la penca del nopal aliñada, junto con otras sustancias, ayuda a aliviar y curar toda clase de quemaduras. El agua de cocimiento del nopal se utiliza también como vermífugo y diurético, contra las lombrices intestinales y la inflamación de la vejiga. Para el primer fin se toma en dosis elevadas: obra como laxante y expulsa los parásitos. Las pencas del nopal, cortadas por la mitad y calentadas, se emplean en ciertos casos como cataplasmas para favorecer la madurez de los abscesos y descongestionarlos.

A esta planta se le han encontrado propiedades expectorantes y antipiréticas en casos de gripe; de acuerdo con numerosas investigaciones, ayuda a expulsar las flemas y a bajar la fiebre.

Obesidad. Se ha puesto de moda que en todas las dietas se tome un jugo de nopal con naranja o alguna otra fruta. Esto se fundamenta en que gracias a la gran cantidad de fibra que tiene esta planta, ayuda retardar el tiempo en que se absorben los nutrimentos y entran a la sangre y por lo tanto facilita su eliminación. También, las fibras insolubles que contiene, crean una sensación de saciedad, haciendo que disminuya el hambre de las personas y ayudan a una buena digestión. Así mismo, las proteínas vegetales promueven la movilización de líquidos en el torrente sanguíneo, disminuyéndose la celulitis y la retención de líquidos.

Diabetes e hiperglucemia. También se habla que ayuda a las personas que padecen diabetes. El nopal incrementa los niveles y la sensibilidad a la insulina logrando con esto estabilizar y regular el nivel de azúcar en la sangre. Se ha comprobado científicamente el poder hipoglucemiante del nopal, es decir, como un efectivo tratamiento para la prevención de la diabetes. Se han llevado a cabo investigaciones en el Instituto Politécnico Nacional, donde se documenta que el nopal disminuye las concentraciones de glucosa en sangre. En estos estudios se ha demostrado que la ingestión de nopal antes de cada alimento, durante diez días, provoca la disminución del peso corporal y reduce las concentraciones de glucosa, colesterol y triglicéridos en sangre. Esto se ha visto solamente en personas que son resistentes a la insulina, o sea en pacientes con diabetes tipo II, pero para las personas que tienen diabetes tipo I (que no producen insulina), el consumo de nopal no sustituye las inyecciones de ésta.

Colesterol. En personas con colesterol elevado se ha demostrado que el consumo de nopal ayuda a eliminarlo, evitando que se absorba gran parte de éste y así no se acumule en venas y arterias. Los aminoácidos, la fibra y la niacina contenidos en el nopal previenen que el exceso de azúcar en la sangre se convierta en grasa, mientras que por otro lado, actúa metabolizando la grasa y los ácidos grasos, reduciendo así el colesterol. Se cree que el contenido de LDL (lipoproteína de baja densidad) en el nopal es la principal causa de que el colesterol sea expulsado del cuerpo, ya que las LDL actúan a nivel del hígado removiendo y retirando el colesterol que el cuerpo tiene en exceso. Al mismo tiempo se ha visto que esta cantidad de LDL no afecta a las HDL (lipoproteínas de alta densidad) o colesterol "bueno". El nopal tiene una cantidad suficiente de aminoácidos y fibra, incluyendo los antioxidantes vitaminas C y A, los cuales previenen la posibilidad de daños en las paredes de los vasos sanguíneos, así como también la formación de plaquetas de grasa, y es así como también tiene una propiedad preventiva en relación a la aterosclerosis.

Propiedad de antibiótico. Los nopales tienen antibióticos naturales; esta propiedad está relacionada con el metabolismo ácido crasuláceo (CAM) de las plantas, el cual, en las cactáceas; inhibe o suspende el crecimiento de varias especies bacterianas. De ahí que tanto el consumo del nopal como la aplicación de cataplasmas de pencas de nopal tengan efectos benéficos en heridas e infecciones de la piel.

Cáncer. En un experimento realizado con ratones con tumores cancerígenos, se administraron extractos acuosos de Opuntia máxima (sustancia que se encuentra en el nopal) y se encontró la prolongación del periodo de latencia de dichos tumores malignos. No curó el cáncer, pero lo detuvo. Aún no se sabe la causa, pero se están realizando varios estudios al respecto.

Desórdenes gastrointestinales y digestión. Por último, se sabe que las fibras vegetales y los mucílagos controlan el exceso de ácidos gástricos y protegen la mucosa gastrointestinal, previniendo así las úlceras gástricas y todo ese tipo de afecciones. El nopal contiene vitaminas A y C, complejo B, minerales: Calcio, Magne-sio, Sodio, Potasio, Hierro y fibras en lignina, celulosa, hemicelulosa, pectina y mucílagos que en conjunto con los 17 aminoácidos ayudan a eliminar toxinas. Las toxinas ambientales provocadas por el alcohol y el humo del cigarro que inhiben el sistema inmunológico del cuerpo, son eliminadas por el nopal. También limpia el colon, ya que contiene fibras dietéticas solubles e insolubles. Las fibras dietéticas insolubles absorben agua y aceleran el paso de los alimentos por el tracto digestivo, y contribuyen a regular el movimiento intestinal, además, la presencia de las fibras insolubles en el colon ayuda a diluir la concentración de cancerígenos que pudieran estar presentes.

Uso medicinal

El nopal es una verdura altamente solicitada por el pueblo de México desde tiempos prehispánicos, no solamente por la ricura de su sabor, sino por sus bondades para la salud.

Además de un alimento sabroso, sólo o combinado con cualquier platillo, el nopal es un remedio muy eficaz para el tratamiento de diversas enfermedades como la diabetes.

El nopal ha cobrado una particular importancia en la medicina por sus propiedades hipoglucemiantes.

Es rico en calcio, potasio y fósforo, sodio, vitamina C y fibra vegetal. Y tiene usos medicinales para la gripe, las quemaduras, las inflamaciones de la vejiga y otros padecimientos.

Además, es un buen remedio contra la gastritis y los cólicos intestinales. Se utiliza para las afecciones de los pulmones.

El agua de cocimiento del nopal se utiliza también como vermífugo y diurético, contra las lombrices intestinales y la inflamación de la vejiga.

Las pencas cortadas por la mitad y calentadas, se emplean en ciertos casos como cataplasmas para favorecer la madurez de los abscesos y descongestionarlos.

Tiene propiedades expectorantes y antipiréticas en casos de gripe y ayuda a expulsar las flemas y a bajar la fiebre.

Además se están estudiando sus beneficios para la cosmeatría.

Para la obesidad

En el exceso de peso, puede servir como complemento por la gran calidad de fibra que contiene, se expande en el estomago y disminuye significativamente el apetito. El mayor logro se alcanza tomándolo quince minutos antes de los alimentos.

Para el estreñimiento

Por su condición en fibra y al rehidratarse, estimula los movimientos normales del intestino, corrigiendo el estreñimiento, además evita o alivia las hemorroides.

Para la diabetes

Contiene encimas y actúa como la insulina, ayudando a que el azúcar pueda penetrar a las células para que sea sintetizada y los niveles de glucosa se mantengan normales.

Algunas de las formas en que se puede utilizar con fines medicinales sería licuado junto con media naranja, piña y perejil. Pero para un tratamiento prolongado, esto quizás sería molesto, por eso hemos fabricado uno de los productos que, en mi opinión, más beneficios nos darán a la salud.

Hablo nada menos que del extracto de nopal con la formula de la micro dosis, que lo hace más potente y fácil de usar; sólo tiene que agregar treinta gotas del extracto de nopal en un jugo de naranja y tomarlo dos veces al día.

Como emoliente

Las pencas contienen abundante mucílago y celulosa, lo que las hace ser emolientes. Se usan en cataplasma para curara heridas, contusiones e irritaciones de la piel.

Los antiguos indígenas ya usaban las palas del nopal como cataplasmas para curar heridas y contusiones. Los colonizadores lo llevaron a España, donde se extendió rápidamente por toda la costa mediterránea.

Indicaciones

Los frutos son astringentes, y dan buen resultado para cortar las diarreas veraniegas. Su jugo se usa en jarabe, como calmante de la tos.

Las flores son diuréticas y antiespasmódicas, y se usan en caso de oliguria (escasa producción de orina) y cistitis.

Preparación y empleo

Uso interno. Los frutos se deben pelar con precaución para no tocarlos con los dedos, pues sus numerosísimas púas se clavan con mucha facilidad y resultan difíciles de quitar. Se pueden tomar frescos o en jarabe.

Jarabe: se prepara cortando los frutos en rodajas y cubriéndolas con azúcar morena. Unas diez horas después se extrae el jarabe (el líquido resultante), pasándolo por un colador para apartar las semillas. Se toma caliente, a cucharadas.

Infusión: con 20 o 30 gramos de flores por litro de agua. Se ingieren tres o cuatro tazas al día.

Uso externo. Cataplasma: las pencas se parten por la mitad, se calientan un poco al horno y se aplican directamente sobre la zona de piel afectada.

El nopal como alimento

Las variedades comestibles se encuentran aclimatadas en casi toda América, desde Canadá hasta Argentina y pueden crecer hasta 4.7 metros de altura. Los misioneros que llegaron al Nuevo Mundo calificaron al nopal de planta "monstruosa", lo que no impidió que viajara a Europa. Sin embargo, en muchos países se desconocen sus virtudes gastronómicas y medicinales y solamente son aprovechados sus frutos, que en España denominan higos chumbos y en México, tunas. Los indígenas prehispánicos de México criaban en las nopaleras la cochinilla de grana, un insecto del que se extraía uno de los colorantes para tejidos más apreciados en el mundo entero y que posteriormente fue empleado también en perfumería.

El nopal es un alimento excelente, rico en sales de calcio (100 gramos proporcionan 96 miligramos) y de potasio, especialmente sulfatos y oxalatos, fósforo, sodio, vitamina C y fibra vegetal. Las hojas del nopal, que una vez cortadas y aliñadas reciben el nombre de nopalitos, se comen en una gran variedad de platillos, tales como las ensaladas acompañadas de cebolla, limón, chile y aceite de oliva. También se consumen asadas, con huevos ahogados, cebolla, ajo, chile frito y cilantro, y de muchas otras maneras. Los nopalitos figuran como ingrediente en diversos platillos típicos de la cocina mexicana: nopalitos con charales, "indios vestidos", revoltijo, nopalitos navegantes y mixiotes de pollo, por ejemplo.

A pesar de que el nopal es un alimento con un alto grado de humedad, su contenido de fibra en base seca es muy importante ya que su contenido como fibra dietética es mayor al 20% guardando una relación 30:70 de fibra soluble a insoluble. Ante esto y su fácil preparación para el consumo humano se pueden desarrollar alimentos ricos en fibra, ya que se han comprobado los beneficios que ocasiona su consumo por medio de investigaciones que relacionan el consumo de fibra y la disminución de padecimientos como cáncer de colon, arterosclerosis y diabetes entre otros.

El polvo de nopal que no es otra cosa más que nopal deshidratado y molido, ha venido a ofrecer una solución tanto para este inconveniente, como también para la elaboración de una gama más amplia de productos tales como dulces, panes, galletas, tostadas, tortillas, etc.

Así que ya lo sabe: cocido, asado con jitomate, chile y cebolla, en una rica sopa, relleno de queso, o aprovechando sus deliciosos frutos en helados, aguas frescas y dulces de tuna, el nopal siempre debe estar presente en la dieta de su familia.

Bebidas

Agua de nopal

Ingredientes:

3 nopales medianos
2 rebanadas de piña
1 litro de agua
Azúcar al gusto
2 limones

Preparación:

Se lavan perfectamente los nopales y se parten en tiras pequeñas. Las rebanadas de piña se parten en pedazos medianos. Se ponen los nopales y la piña en el agua y se licua hasta que se desintegren por completo. Se le agrega el jugo de los dos limones después de licuar, al igual que el azúcar al gusto.

Jugo de toronja, naranja y nopal

Ingredientes:

2 tazas de jugo de toronja
1½ tazas de jugo de naranja

¼ de taza de nopales partidos en tiritas

Miel al gusto

Preparación:

Combine todos los ingredientes en la licuadora y licue a velocidad rápida. Si lo desea, antes de servir puede añadir unos cubitos de hielo.

Da para aproximadamente seis porciones.

Naranja con nopal y piña

Ingredientes:

1 vaso de jugo de naranja

1 rebanada de piña

2 nopales pequeños

1 cucharada de miel de abeja

Preparación:

Lave y ralle los nopales y déjelos reposando toda la noche; en la mañana se pican.

Corte el trozo de piña que necesita

Coloque en la licuadora los nopales junto con el jugo de naranja recién hecho y la miel. Procese hasta que la mezcla sea uniforme (a velocidad baja). Se continúa licuando hasta que la mezcla esté suave.

Nota: Este jugo se toma de preferencia en ayunas y sin colar para aprovechar la fibra que contiene.

Licuado de nopal

Ingredientes:

¼ de taza de pepino sin cáscara

¼ de taza de chayote sin espinas con cáscara

1 nopal limpio

1 naranja (jugo)

½ taza de piña

½ taza de agua

Preparación:

Licuar todos los ingredientes, uno a uno.

Tomarlo con el desayuno, sin colar.

¡Disfrute su efecto y su sabor!

Jugo de nopal, limón y sábila

(Para diabéticos)

Ingredientes:

3 limones

1 nopal

½ taza de agua purificada

2 dientes de ajo

1 pedacito de sábila fresca

Preparación:

Lavar los limones, el nopal y la sábila, quitarle a ésta las espinitas de las orillas.

Extraer el jugo de los limones.

Pelar los ajos.

Licuar todos los ingredientes perfectamente.

Servir en un vaso y tomarlo inmediatamente.

Nota: Este jugo se toma durante una semana, se descansa ocho días y se vuelve a tomar una semana más.

Jugo de nopal

(Para dolores menstruales)

Ingredientes:

1 naranja

½ nopal

2 trozos de sábila

¼ de limón sin cáscara

20 mililitros de agua mineral.

Preparación:

Verter en la licuadora los ingredientes. Mezclar y tomar sin colar en ayunas, durante los cinco días previos al inicio de tu periodo.

Licuado de piña, apio, toronja y nopal

(Para quemar grasa)

Ingredientes:

1 rebanada de piña

2 ramas de apio

2 toronjas

½ nopalito

1 cucharada de miel de abeja

Preparación:

Lavar y desinfectar perfectamente la fruta y la verdura.

Extraer el jugo de las toronjas.

En el extractor de jugos pasar la piña, el apio y el nopalito.

Al terminar, agregarle el de toronja y la cucharita de miel.

Mezclar todo y beberlo enseguida para que se puedan aprovechar todos sus nutrientes.

Función del jugo:

Este jugo es rico en fibra, es depurativo, diurético, ayuda a eliminar grasa y toxinas, mejora el metabolismo de las proteínas, evita la aparición de la celulitis, y por si esto fuera poco, combate también el dolor reumático y artrítico. Se necesita beber este jugo durante siete días en ayunas para que se vean mejor los resultados, recordar que cada organismo es diferente y el peso que cada persona pierde es variable, por lo que no se debe olvidar incluir en la dieta diaria agua, frutas y verduras para que se pueda quemar grasa más fácilmente.

Atole de nopal

Ingredientes:

2 litros de leche

Piloncillo al gusto

2 rajitas de canela

Vainilla al gusto

200 gramos de masa "como la de las tortillas"

1½ taza de agua

10 nopales cocidos y lavados

Preparación:

Hervir la leche con el piloncillo, la canela y la vainilla; cuando esté hirviendo agregar la masa que fue anteriormente disuelta y colada en una taza de agua.

Dejar en fuego bajo hasta que espese. Moler los nopales e incorporar a la leche, mezclar, dejar hervir, verificar el sabor y servir.

Jugo de nopal y naranja

(Para la gripe)

Ingredientes:

1 nopal chico

4 naranjas

Preparación:

Lavar perfectamente los ingredientes.

Extraer el jugo de las naranjas y licuarlo con el nopal. Servir y tomar de inmediato.

Jugo de nopal y menta

(Para problemas intestinales)

Ingredientes:

1 nopal

1 rama de menta

1 cucharadita de miel

1 vaso de agua

Preparación:

Pasar el nopal y la rama de menta por el extractor.

Mezclar el jugo con el agua y la miel. Servir y tomar de inmediato.

Ensaladas

Nopalitos en ensalada

Ingredientes:

6 nopalitos tiernos

½ queso fresco desmenuzado

2 chiles serranos picados

¼ cebolla, picada finamente

3 ramitas de cilantro picado

½ cucharada de orégano molido

5 cucharadas de vinagre

2 cucharadas de aceite de oliva

Sal y pimienta

Preparación:

Lavar bien los nopales y partirlos en tiritas.

Cocinarlos en agua con un poco de sal y luego escurrir y lavarlos con agua fría.

Añadir a los nopalitos el vinagre, aceite, cilantro, orégano, la cebolla, los chiles, la sal y pimienta.

Revolver todo muy bien y espolvorear con el queso desmenuzado.

Ensalada de nopales

Ingredientes:

1 kilo de nopales

1 cebolla partida por la mitad

4 tazas de agua

2 cucharaditas de sal

2 jitomates grandes cortados al gusto

1 cebolla cortada para ensalada

4 chiles verdes cortados

Preparación:

Limpiar los nopales y quitarles todas las espinas con cuidado.

Una vez limpios se cortan en tiras, luego se cuecen durante unos cuarenta y cinco minutos en agua hirviendo con la cebolla partida por la mitad y la sal.

Transcurrido este tiempo se escurren y se mezclan con el resto de ingredientes, sazonando al gusto.

Ensalada de nopalitos

Ingredientes:

10 nopalitos tiernos y limpios

2 jitomates rebanados

1 manojito de cilantro picado

1 cebolla mediana en rodajas

2 aguacates

¼ de queso fresco

Jugo de limón al gusto

Aceite de oliva, el necesario

Sal al gusto.

Preparación:

Cocer los nopalitos. Cortarlos en trocitos delgados y alargaditos. Dejarlos reposar para que se les salga un poco la viscosidad y escurrir muy bien. Adornar con el cilantro, la cebolla, el jitomate, el aguacate y el queso. Sazonar con el aceite de oliva, el jugo de limón y la sal.

Ensalada picante de nopal

Ingredientes:

15 nopales limpios y tiernos cortados en tiras

10 cáscaras de tomate verde

4 cucharadas de vinagre

½ taza de aceite de oliva

½ cebolla para quitar la baba del nopal

½ cebolla en rajitas

1 aguacate en rajas sin cáscaras

1 jitomate en rodajas finas

1 taza de cilantro limpio y picado

6 chiles de árbol limpios y fritos sin semillas

2 tazas de queso parmesano rallado

2 cucharadas de orégano

2½ tazas de agua

Preparación:

En una olla con agua se cuecen los nopales, media cebolla, las cáscaras de tomate para cortar la viscosidad del nopal y sal al gusto.

Se hierve treinta minutos hasta que los nopales estén a punto suave.

Se cuelan y se apartan la cebolla y las cáscaras de tomate; en una ensaladera se mezclan bien las rajitas de cebolla, orégano, vinagre, aceite de oliva y el chile de árbol en trozos; aún estando los nopales calientes se ponen a marinar en la ensalada.

Ensalada de nopales tricolor

Ingredientes:

10 nopales cocidos y cortados en cuadritos

½ kg de chicharrón en trozos

1 ramito de cilantro, lavado y picado

3 chiles verdes lavados, picados y asados

2 jitomates lavados y asados

½ cebolla asada (finamente picada)

1 aguacate para adornar

Sal al gusto

Preparación:

Revuelva todos los ingredientes en una ensaladera, cuidando de que todo quede finamente picado, y al momento de servir acompañe con el aguacate.

Sazone al gusto, sirva con tortillas calientes.

Ensalada de nopales con sardina

Ingredientes:

6 nopales cocidos (partidos en cuadritos)

1 lata de sardinas en aceite

2 jitomates cortados en gajos

2 huevos cocidos en rebanadas

½ taza de mayonesa

1 aguacate rebanado

3 papas cocidas (cortadas en juliana)

200 gramos de queso añejo rallado

Sal y pimienta al gusto

Preparación:

Coloque los nopales en un platón, agregue las sardinas escurridas, sin piel, ni espinas.

Añada las papas, jitomate, aguacate y huevo.

Revuelva todo con la mayonesa y el queso, sazonado previamente con sal y pimienta.

Ensalada de nopales y rabanitos

Ingredientes:

2 kilos de nopales cocidos y picados

1 kilo de jitomates en rodajas

4 rabanitos

1 manojo de cilantro

5 aguacates en tiras

2 cebollas en ruedas

Vinagre, el necesario

Aceite de oliva

Queso picado

Rodajas de huevo cocido

Sal al gusto

Preparación:

Mezcle todos los ingredientes, excepto las rodajas de huevo cocido y el queso picado.

Sirva adornando con estos últimos ingredientes.

Ensalada de nopales

Ingredientes:

9 nopales grandes

4 cebollas de rabo

2 ramitas de cilantro

4 jitomates grandes

60 gramos de queso añejo

Una pizca de bicarbonato

Un poco de orégano

Sal al gusto

Preparación:

En dos litros de agua ponga las cebollas de rabo finamente picadas.

Cuando el agua empiece a hervir añada los nopales limpios y cortados en cuadritos. Al volver a hervir agregue el bicarbonato. El agua hará efervescencia y cortará la viscosidad (baba) de los nopales.

Ya cocidos los nopales escúrralos bien, poniéndoles una servilleta mojada con agua muy fría. Ya fríos añada los jitomates pelados y partidos en cuadritos.

Sazone con sal, coloque en la ensaladera y adorne con cebolla picada, cilantro, un poco de orégano y el queso añejo.

Ensalada de nopales con tocino

Ingredientes:

2 kilos de nopales cocidos, picados y escurridos

2 kilos de espinacas

¼ de tocino

Pan en cuadritos

1 apio picado

2 huevos cocidos

Aceite de oliva

Vinagre, el necesario

Sal y pimienta al gusto

Preparación:

Lave las espinacas, dore el tocino y un poco de pan en la grasa del tocino. Espolvoree la ensaladera con apio molido.

Mezcle estos ingredientes con las espinacas crudas, los nopales, el vinagre, el aceite de oliva, sal y pimienta.

Adorne con ruedas de huevo cocido.

Ensalada de nopales con cebollitas

Ingredientes:

2 kilos de nopales cocidos, picados y escurridos

1 kilo de ejotes cocidos y picados en trocitos

3 jitomates rebanados

3 rábanos grandes

1 cebolla mediana en rebanadas finas

Chiles poblanos en rajas al gusto

Cilantro al gusto

Aceite de oliva, el necesario

2 cucharadas de vinagre

Queso rallado al gusto

Preparación:

En una ensaladera ponga los nopales, los ejotes, la cebolla, los chiles poblanos y el cilantro.

Mezcle con aceite de oliva, vinagre, jitomate y rábanos. Adorne y sirva con queso rallado.

Ensalada de nopales y aguacate

Ingredientes:

10 nopales limpios y tiernos

1 cebolla morada

1 cucharadita de orégano en polvo

Aceite de oliva

Cilantro bien picadito al gusto

2 jitomates en rebanadas delgadas

Queso añejo rallado al gusto

2 aguacates en rebanadas

Sal de grano al gusto

Preparación:

En una olla ponga a cocer los nopalitos cortados en cuadritos. Agregue sal de grano.

Pase los nopales a un colador y escúrralos bien.

En una ensaladera mezcle todo y adorne con el jitomate, el aguacate y el queso.

Ensalada de nopales en tacos

Ingredientes:

15 nopales cocidos y picados

1 cebolla picada

3 ramas de cilantro finamente picado

5 dientes de ajo picado

3 chiles serranos picados

½ cucharada de consomé

1 cucharadita de orégano

2 cucharadas de aceite

2 cucharadas de vinagre

Sal y pimienta al gusto

Preparación:

Mezcle todos los ingredientes muy bien y sazone. Sirva en tacos.

Ensalada de nopales y germinado

Ingredientes:

½ kilo de nopales previamente cocidos

4 jitomates en cubos

½ cebolla morada finamente picada

Aceite de oliva al gusto

3 limones, el jugo

1 pizca de sal

Pimienta negra al gusto

Hojas de lechuga para servir

Germinado de alfalfa al gusto

250 gramos de queso fresco en cubos

2 aguacates en rebanadas

Preparación:

Picar el jitomate, la cebolla y los nopales previamente cocidos. Mezclar con el aderezo y dejar marinar por dos horas. Para el aderezo mezclar el aceite con el jugo de limón, aceite de oliva, sal y pimienta. Servir sobre hojas de lechuga, germinado de trigo, la ensalada de nopales y decorar con cuadritos de queso fresco y aguacate en rebanadas.

Ensalada de nopal y tuna

Ingredientes:

2 jitomates bola

½ cebolla

4 chiles de árbol frescos

4 tunas rojas

8 nopales tiernos

1 taza de queso cotija

1 limón (jugo)

Sal y pimienta

Tostadas horneadas para acompañar

Preparación:

Picar los jitomates, cebolla y chiles. Colocar en un tazón y revolver con el queso cotija.

Cocer los nopales. Picar los nopales fríos y las tunas. Revolver con los demás ingredientes. Servir y acompañar con tostadas y espolvorear queso adicional.

Ensalada de nopales y jícama

Ingredientes:

6 nopales

Aceite de maíz

Sal y pimienta

1 jícama

¼ de taza de jugo de limón

3 cucharadas de vinagre de vino tinto

½ taza de aceite de olivo

2 jitomates

1 aguacate

Berros cocidos

Preparación:

Los nopales, los cortaremos. En una sartén bien caliente se saltean por dos o tres minutos, con un poco de aceite, sazonándolos con sal y pimienta al gusto. Después los retiramos del fuego y los dejamos reposar. La jícama se pela y se ralla. Se marina en un cuarto de taza de jugo de limón, y se sazona con sal, la dejamos reposar por una hora. En un recipiente se mezclan el vino tinto y el aceite de olivo, muy poco a poco, sin dejar de mover. Le añadimos sal y pimienta al gusto (si no se consigue vinagre de vino tinto, bastará con evaporar el alcohol del vino tinto a fuego lento, y acidificar con vinagre y unas gotas de limón). Los jitomates y el aguacate se cortan en rebanadas delgadas.

Para emplatar, se pone la jícama en un moldecito circular (como una lata de atún), al centro del plato, presionando un poco. Después colocamos el molde sobre un plato, vaciando la jícama con cuidado para que no pierda la forma. Se decora con un poco de nopales alrededor. Agregamos el jitomate y el aguacate. También añadimos los berros —sólo las puntas— bien lavados. Para finalizar, se mezcla la vinagreta y se baña con ella la ensalada.

Cóctel de nopales y aguacate

Ingredientes:

400 gramos de aguacate cortado en cuadros

400 gramos de nopales cocidos en cuadros

8 cucharadas de cebolla, finamente picada

8 cucharadas de cilantro, finamente picado

Chiles serranos, picados al gusto

Hojas de lechuga (adorno)

Aderezo:

½ de taza yogurt

4 cucharadas de mayonesa

3 cucharadas de salsa inglesa

2 cucharadas de salsa catsup

Sal al gusto

Preparación:

Se colocan en un tazón el aguacate, los nopales, cebolla, cilantro y chiles serranos.

Se añade el aderezo y se mezcla. Se sirve en platitos o copas para coctel y se adorna con hojas de lechuga.

Preparación del aderezo:

Se mezclan todos los ingredientes y se sirve.

Sopas

Crema de nopalitos

Ingredientes:

1½ kilogramos de nopales

1 cebolla

3 dientes de ajo

1 taza de crema de leche

300 gramos de escamoles

Sal

Pimienta

Manteca

Preparación:

Cortar en trozos las pencas de nopal y hervirlas en agua salada durante treinta y cinco minutos. Freír la cebolla picada junto con los dientes de ajo picados. Moler esta preparación con los nopales bien escurridos en caldo de verdura agregando la crema.

Hervir durante veinte minutos y agregar sal y pimienta al gusto. Agregar los escamoles (huevos de hormiga).

Sopa de nopal con pollo

Ingredientes:

8 nopales

1 cebolla, en gajos

5 rebanadas de tocino

250 gramos de queso fresco

1 pellizco de orégano

3 chiles chipotles, picados

3 piezas de pollo (pierna, muslo y rabadilla)

1 zanahoria

2 ramas de apio

2 dientes de ajo

2 litros de agua

1 cucharada de consomé en polvo

Preparación:

Se lavan y se cortan en pequeños cuadros los nopales y se ponen a hervir durante veinte minutos, aproximadamente. Una vez cocidos, se lavan con agua fría, para quitarles la baba.

Para elaborar el caldo de pollo, en dos litros de agua se colocan las piezas de pollo junto con la zanahoria, la cebolla en trozos, las ramas de apio, dos dientes de ajo, los chiles chipotles y una cucharada de consomé en polvo. Se deja hervir hasta que el pollo esté cocido. Se sacan las piezas y el caldo se cuela. Las piezas de pollo se desmenuzan.

En una sartén se ponen a freír las rebanadas de tocino y una vez que estén doraditas se sacan y se colocan en un papel absorbente y se trituran. En el mismo aceite del tocino se ponen a freír los gajos de cebolla hasta que se blanqueen, y se retiran de la sartén.

En una olla se coloca el caldo de pollo colado y se le agregan los nopales, el tocino en trocitos, la cebolla y el pollo desmenuzado. Se deja cocinar diez minutos y se le agrega el orégano y el queso cortado en cuadritos. Se deja un minuto y estará lista para servirse.

Sopa de nopales

Ingredientes:

500 gramos puré de jitomate

100 gramos de cebolla en cuadritos

2 cucharadas de harina

800 gramos de nopales cocidos

1 litro de caldo de res

1 cucharadita de orégano

Sal y pimienta

Aceite vegetal

Queso Oaxaca, panela o fresco

Crema fresca

Preparación:

En una cazuela calentar dos cucharadas de aceite y freír la cebolla hasta que se transparente.

Agregar la harina y mover rápido hasta integrarla.

Agregar el puré de jitomate, sazonar con sal, pimienta y orégano. Cuando comience a espesar poner el caldo de res y rectificar la sazón. Integrar los nopales cocidos y lavados y dejar que hierva diez minutos.

Para servir poner en los platos el queso y la crema y verter la sopa muy caliente para que el queso se derrita.

Sopa azteca de nopales

Ingredientes:

20 nopales cocidos y finamente picados

1 barra de mantequilla

Chiles poblanos en rajas, al gusto

2 elotes desgranados tiernitos

5 jitomates molidos

Cebolla y ajo al gusto

¼ de crema agria

Sal y pimienta al gusto

Preparación:

En una cacerola ponga la mantequilla. Acitrone las rajas de chile poblano y los granos de elote. Cuando estén transparentes añada el jitomate molido, la cebolla, el ajo y los nopales picados.

Deje hervir hasta que estén cocidas las verduras.

Agregue crema; la sopa debe quedar caldosa. Sirva caliente.

Coditos y nopales

Ingredientes:

3 nopales medianos

1 paquete de pasta tipo codito

½ barrita de margarina

¼ de taza de leche

¾ de taza de crema

½ cucharadita de pimienta

½ cucharadita de hierbas finas

2 cucharaditas de consomé de pollo en polvo

¾ de taza de queso parmesano

Preparación:

Corte los nopales en cuadritos, enjuáguelos y cuézalos en suficiente agua; escúrralos.

Cueza la pasta en litro y medio de agua, hasta que esté *al dente*; escúrrala y póngala en un tazón.

Agregue la margarina y mézclela con cuidado para no romper la pasta.

Licue juntos la leche, crema, pimienta, hierbas finas y consomé.

Vacíe sobre la pasta, añada los nopales y espolvoree el queso.

Sopa de nopales

Ingredientes:

1 jitomate molido

5 nopales picados

1 chile morita

4 dientes de ajo (1 para el caldillo)

1 cebolla pequeña

1 litro de caldo de carne de res o pollo

Queso panela

Preparación:

Se cuecen los nopales en su propio líquido. Para ello se ponen en una cacerola sin agua y sin nada para que suelten su propio líquido y se vaya consumiendo con el calor al tiempo que se cuecen los nopales.

Freír mientras los ajos y el chile morita partidos por mitades. Agregar el jitomate cuando estén dorados y también la cebolla. Una vez sofritos pasarlos por un colador.

Freír nuevamente unos minutos y añadir el caldillo, la sal y los nopales. Dejar que hiervan hasta que estén suaves.

Otras versiones de la sopa de nopales incorporan huevo cocido encima a la hora de servirla.

También es costumbre servir la sopa de nopales con muchos complementos: rábanos, lechuga, cebolla picada, orégano, chiles, el limón y carnes rebanadas, tortillas, tostadas, etc. De forma que se convierte en un plato muy suculento.

Sopa de nopales y habas

Ingredientes:

4 nopales cocidos cortados en cuadros

8 tomates verdes

1 trozo de cebolla

1 diente de ajo

1 taza de habas tiernas

4 chiles verdes enteros

2 tazas de caldo de pollo

4 ramitas de cilantro finamente picado

3 ramas de epazote finamente picado

1 cucharada de aceite

Preparación:

En una cazuela caliente el aceite, vacíe los tomates previamente molidos con cebolla y ajo, agregue las habas y los chiles enteros para sazonar con sal. Vacíe el caldo de pollo y deje hervir hasta que las habas estén cocidas. Agregue los nopales y deje hervir durante cinco minutos.

Agregue el epazote, el cilantro y sirva caliente.

Sopa caldosa de nopales

Ingredientes:

10 nopales cocidos finamente picados

1 litro de caldo de pollo

1 barra de mantequilla

3 chiles poblanos en rajas

Huevos suavemente batidos

1 ajo

1 trocito de cebolla

5 jitomates molidos

Preparación:

Una vez caliente la mantequilla agregue la cebolla, el ajo, el jitomate picado y las rajas de chile.

Una vez sazonado añada el caldo y los nopales. Al hervir agregue los huevos y mueva hasta que se desbaraten. La sopa debe estar caldosa y bien caliente.

Sopa de charales

Ingredientes:

6 nopales cocidos y cortados en rajas

6 tomates verdes

2 cucharadas de cilantro picado

½ kilo de charales secos

½ cebolla

3 chiles verdes serranos

1 cubo de consomé de pollo

Aceite, el necesario

Sal al gusto

Preparación:

Muela los tomates cocidos con cebolla, agua y consomé de pollo.

Fría la salsa en aceite caliente, agregue sal y deje sazonar por unos minutos con un poco de consomé de pollo en polvo.

Agregue los nopales, los charales y los chiles en rajas, añada seis tazas de agua; rectifique la sazón y finalmente agregue el cilantro y sirva caliente.

Sopa de nopal al minuto

Ingredientes:

10 nopales cocidos cortados en cuadritos

2 litros de caldo de pollo

1 rama de epazote

3 chiles chipotles

Preparación:

Hierva los nopales en el caldo de pollo junto con el epazote durante cinco minutos.

Añada el chile chipotle, hierva por unos minutos más y listo.

Sopa de camarón y nopales

Ingredientes:

20 nopales cocidos finamente picados

1 lata de chiles chipotles

1 diente de ajo

½ cebolla

½ kilo de jitomate (bien molido)

1 rama de perejil

Camarón cocido

4 tazas de agua para el condimento

Aceite, el necesario

Preparación:

Una vez caliente el aceite, sazone el jitomate con el ajo y la cebolla molidos.

Añada el caldo de camarón, los chiles chipotles, los nopales y la rama de perejil.

Caldo de nopales con habas

Ingredientes:

8 nopales picados y cocidos

¼ de kilo de habas secas y peladas

1 cucharadita de consomé de pollo en polvo
Cebolla, ajo y cilantro
¼ de cucharada de aceite
Sal al gusto

Preparación:

Ponga a hervir las habas hasta que casi se deshagan, agregue la cebolla y ajo previamente acitronados en el aceite caliente.

Escurra los nopales y agréguelos a las habas junto con el cilantro, la sal y el consomé de pollo en polvo hasta que hierva durante diez minutos.

Sirva acompañado con rebanadas de pan frito.

Sopa de nopal

Ingredientes:

2 dientes de ajo picados

3 cucharadas de cebolla picada

1 cucharada de aceite de maíz o girasol

6 tazas de caldo de pollo hecho en casa

9 nopales cortados en cuadros

1 manojo de cilantro

1 chile chipotle

Una pizca de sal

Pimienta al gusto

1 pechuga de pollo cortada en cuadros

2 papas medianas picadas

2 zanahorias cortadas en cuadros pequeños

Preparación:

En una olla grande freír el ajo y la cebolla con la cantidad de aceite indicada. Agregar el caldo de pollo, los nopales, el cilantro y el chile.

Poner a hervir, añadir la sal y la pimienta. Agregar el pollo, las papas y las zanahorias. Cocinar a fuego lento durante una hora o hasta que el pollo esté blando.

Sopa de lentejas con nopales

Ingredientes:

6 nopales cocidos y picados

1 taza de lentejas

1 trozo de cebolla

½ cebolla rebanada

2 dientes de ajo

2 jitomates molidos

3 ramitas de cilantro

5 tazas de agua o caldo

2 cucharadas de aceite

Sal al gusto

Preparación:

Lave bien las lentejas y déjelas remojando en agua o caldo.

En ese mismo líquido póngalas a cocer con un diente de ajo, un pedazo de cebolla y una cucharadita de sal.

En una cacerola con poco aceite, fría el otro diente de ajo y la cebolla rebanada; cuando ésta tome un color transparente, añada el jitomate molido y colado.

En seguida añada los nopales y el cilantro picado, pruebe de sal y deje cocinando tapado a fuego suave por cuarenta minutos aproximadamente o hasta que las lentejas estén cocidas.

Crema fría de nopal y cerveza

Ingredientes:

4 nopales pelados y picados

½ taza de crema ácida

1 cerveza clara

½ cucharadita de azúcar

1 cucharadita de cilantro finamente picado

¼ de cucharadita de pimienta

½ cucharadita de sal

Preparación:

Mezcle la crema ácida con la cerveza, añada los nopales picados, sal, azúcar, pimienta y licue todo lo anterior.

Agregue el cilantro picado y refrigere.

Nopales en crema de espinacas

Ingredientes:

20 nopales cocidos finamente picados

3 kilos de espinacas cocidas

5 jitomates

Cebolla y ajo al gusto

Chiles al gusto

1 barrita de mantequilla

Preparación:
Ponga los jitomates molidos, la cebolla y el ajo en la mantequilla caliente.
Añada el agua de las espinacas, los chiles y los nopales. Sirva bien caliente.

Nopales en crema de zanahoria

Ingredientes:
20 nopales finamente picados
1 kilo de zanahorias (en jugo)
10 zanahorias finamente picadas
1 barra de mantequilla
1 cebolla
1 diente de ajo
3 jitomates
1 litro de caldo de pollo

Preparación:
Agregue a la mantequilla derretida el jugo de las zanahorias, los nopales, las zanahorias y el caldo de pollo.
Muela el jitomate con el ajo y la cebolla, añada a la mezcla anterior y deje sazonar por espacio de diez minutos. Sirva con queso rallado.

Crema de nopales

Ingredientes:
20 nopales finamente picados
1 barra de mantequilla
5 papas grandes cocidas, en puré

½ kilo de jitomate

1 paquete de galletas saladas

Cebolla y ajo al gusto

1 litro de caldo de pollo

Preparación:

Fría el ajo, la cebolla y el jitomate en la mantequilla. Una vez sazonados añada el caldo de pollo, los nopales, el puré de papa y sazone.

Sirva bien caliente y acompañe con las galletas.

Sopa de nopal

Ingredientes:

4 nopales tiernos

2 dientes de ajo

½ ramita de cilantro

1 cucharadita de consomé de pollo

1 cucharada de aceite de oliva

Preparación:

Picar en cuadritos muy pequeños el ajo, picar el nopal al gusto, picar el cilantro en trozos pequeños.

En un recipiente freír el ajo con el aceite de oliva, añadir el agua y añadir el consomé de pollo.

Esperar el punto de ebullición para añadir el nopal crudo.

Una vez cocido el nopal, no escurrir el caldillo, ahí mismo agregar el cilantro.

Esperar otro hervor y estará listo ya para servirse.

Spaghetti con nopales y champiñones

Ingredientes:

2 paquetes de spaghetti

4 tazas de agua

1 cucharada de aceite vegetal

1 cucharada de mantequilla

1 taza de nopales cortados en cuadritos

1½ taza de champiñones rebanados

6 cucharadas de vino tinto

Sal y pimienta

Preparación:

Cocer la pasta por quince minutos en agua con sal y aceite.

Calentar la mantequilla a fuego bajo y saltear los nopales.

Después de cinco minutos integrar los champiñones y el vino tinto. Dejar cocinar hasta que el vino se evapore y sazonar.

Acompañar el spaghetti con los nopales y champiñones al gusto.

Nopales en su crema

Ingredientes:

20 nopales cocidos y finamente picados

5 jitomates

1 trozo de cebolla

1 diente de ajo

1 cucharada de consomé de pollo
25 gramos de mantequilla
¼ de queso rallado
2 tazas de agua

Preparación:

Una vez caliente la mantequilla, sazone en ella el jitomate, la cebolla, el ajo y dos tazas de agua.

Integre los nopales y el consomé de pollo.

Agregue el queso rallado.

Guisos

Consejos

Un buen consejo es cocer los nopales en una olla de cobre. Calentar el agua hasta que hierva y entonces añadir los nopales con sal. Dejar cocer diez minutos o hasta que se sientan suaves, entonces escurrir y enjuagar con agua fría.

Si no se tiene olla de cobre, añadir una pizca de bicarbonato a los nopales al momento de la cocción.

Ahora bien, si no se tiene olla de cobre ni bicarbonato, se puede probar cocer los nopalitos con agua mineral embotellada. Ésta también hará que conserven un bonito tono verde.

Para evitar que los nopalitos queden babosos al cocerlos, añadir un par de cáscaras de tomate verde al agua de la cocción; una vez que estén tiernos, escurrir y enjuagar con agua fría.

Para rebanar rápidamente los nopales en juliana, tomar el nopal y cortarlo primero por la mitad en forma vertical, después rebanar las mitades horizontalmente en rebanaditas del grueso que se prefiera.

Nopales en escabeche

Ingredientes:

½ kilo de nopales tiernos y cortados al gusto

1 taza de agua

1 taza de vinagre, de preferencia blanco

½ cucharadita de sal

Pimienta entera

Laurel, tomillo y mejorana al gusto

½ cebolla rebanada

2 zanahorias lavadas, peladas y rebanadas

4 dientes de ajo pelados

Chile de árbol al gusto

2 cucharadas de aceite

Utensilios:

Olla con capacidad de dos litros

Coladera

Sartén

Cuchara

Frascos de vidrio esterilizados

Etiqueta adhesiva

Preparación:

En la olla con agua hirviendo se ponen a cocer los nopales y las zanahorias durante tres minutos. Transcurrido este tiempo, se escurren y enjuagan los nopales y las zanahorias.

En la sartén con el aceite caliente, se sancochan a fuego bajo la cebolla, el ajo y el chile de árbol hasta que la cebolla esté transparente.

Se agregan los nopales y las zanahorias.

Aparte se disuelve la sal en el agua y se agrega el vinagre. Esta solución se agrega a los nopales, se incorpora pimienta, laurel, tomillo y mejorana y se deja hervir todo a fuego medio.

En los frascos esterilizados se vierten los nopales en caliente dejando un centímetro de espacio entre la boca del frasco y el producto. Elimine las burbujas que se puedan formar.

Se tapan los frascos muy bien y se dejan enfriar a temperatura ambiente.

Etiquete indicando el nombre del producto, fecha de elaboración y de caducidad.

Duración:

Los nopales elaborados de esta forma tienen un tiempo de vida aproximado de ocho meses.

Recomendaciones:

Se guarda en lugar fresco seco y oscuro.

Una vez abierto el producto, es necesario mantenerlo en refrigeración.

Aproveche que el nopal se encuentra más barato en los meses de junio, julio y agosto.

Huevos con nopal en salsa de chile ancho

Ingredientes:

8 huevos

3 nopales tiernos

1 jitomate maduro

¼ de cebolla

2 dientes de ajo

Sal y pimienta

2 cucharadas de aceite de oliva

3 chiles anchos (secos)

1½ taza de agua

Preparación:

Se ponen a hervir en una taza de agua los chiles y el jitomate (aproximadamente cinco minutos).

Se ponen a cocer en media taza de agua y a fuego bajo los nopales previamente cortados en cuadros con un poco de sal.

Una vez cocidos los chiles y el jitomate se licuan junto con la cebolla y los dientes de ajo y se les agrega la sal y pimienta.

Se baten los huevos y se ponen a cocinar en una sartén con el aceite y los nopales ya cocidos y escurridos.

Una vez cocidos se agrega la salsa y se incorporan bien.

Nopales rellenos

Ingredientes:

12 nopales tiernos

6 rebanadas de queso manchego o panela

¼ de cebolla en trozo

1 diente de ajo

Sal al gusto

½ taza de harina

4 claras

4 yemas

1½ taza de aceite

Preparación:

Se cuecen los nopales en tres tazas de agua con el ajo, la cebolla y la sal. Se escurren.

Coloque sobre cada nopal una rebanada de queso y tres o cuatro gajitos de cebolla. Cúbralos con otra rebanada de nopal. Asegúrelos con palillos de madera. Rocíelos con sal. Cúbralos con la harina por ambos lados.

Bata las claras a punto de turrón. Agregue las yemas y añádales sal.

Pase los nopales enharinados por el huevo batido y fríalos en una cacerola con el aceite caliente.

Sáquelos y escúrralos.

Báñelos con salsa de jitomate cocido.

Nopales navegantes

Preparación:

6 nopales grandes (picados en cuadros)

4 papas cocidas, peladas y picadas en cuadros

1 taza de charales secos

1 ramita de cilantro

1 pizca de sal

2 cubos de caldo de pollo

Para el caldillo:

3 jitomates

½ cebolla

1 ajo

2 chiles serranos (al gusto)

Preparación:

Muela en la licuadora todos los ingredientes para el caldillo, póngalos a hervir y una vez hervidos, agregue los nopales, las papas y los charales con el cilantro, déjelos espesar y acompáñelos con tortillas calientitas. Al caldillo de jitomate agregar agua al gusto dependiendo de qué tan espeso le guste.

Huaraches de nopal

Ingredientes:

2 tazas de harina de maíz

½ taza de harina de trigo

2 tazas de agua

120 gramos de manteca de cerdo o aceite

Frijoles refritos, los necesarios

10 nopales medianos

100 gramos de queso panela rallado

Preparación:

Mezcle las harinas con el agua, trabaje la masa y forme los huaraches con el molde que venden en muchos mercados, con la torteadora o con un rodillo; tienen que quedar alargados y delgados.

Cuézalos en una sartén por ambos lados y fríalos con la manteca o aceite. Retírelos y úntenles los frijoles, agrégueles nopales y queso.

Para adornarlos y para que sepan más sabrosos, agrégueles salsa.

Nopales al ajillo

Ingredientes:

1 o 2 nopales tiernos por persona

Agua

¼ de cebolla

Aceite de oliva

Sal

Ajos finamente picados

Chile seco serrano o de árbol, opcional

Preparación:

Los nopales se cortan finamente en juliana y se ponen a cocer en agua hirviendo con sal y la cebolla. Cuando están suaves se dejan escurriendo en un colador, retirando la cebolla.

Nota: si se cuenta con olla de cobre, es mejor cocer ahí los nopales para que conserven su verdor.

En una sartén se pone a calentar el aceite de oliva, y se dora el ajo. Si se opta por el chile seco, se añade entero. Una vez dorado todo, cuidando de no quemar el ajo, se agregan los nopales, se baja la lumbre y se deja sazonar diez minutos.

Se sirve para acompañar plato fuerte de carne o con arroz para los vegetarianos.

Nopales rellenos

Ingredientes:

6 nopales grandes y carnosos

6 rebanadas de jamón de pierna

6 rebanadas de queso manchego

½ cebolla

2 huevos

2 cucharadas de harina de trigo

Aceite para freír

Sal y pimienta al gusto

Preparación:

Abrir los nopales por el centro, ponerlos a cocer con el trozo de cebolla y un poco de sal por quince minutos. Una vez que estén suaves escurrirlos y secarlos con un papel absorbente, colocar en medio de cada nopal una rebanada de jamón y una de queso.

Cerrar el nopal con un palillo y espolvorearlo con un poco de harina.

Separar las claras de los huevos y batirlas a punto de turrón, agregar las yemas y las dos cucharadas de harina, con una pizca de sal y pimienta.

Cubrir con esta mezcla los nopales uno a uno y freírlos en aceite muy caliente; una vez que doren por ambos lados, escurrirlos.

Se pueden servir acompañados de un guacamole o unos frijoles y una buena salsa.

Huarache de nopal asado con pollo

Ingredientes:

Aceite en aerosol

6 nopales grandes

1 diente de ajo picado

Marinada:

3 cucharadas de adobo de chile chipotle

3 cucharadas de tallos de cilantro picados

3 cucharadas de hojas de cilantro picadas

Pimienta negra al gusto

6 medias pechugas de pollo sin hueso y piel

Aceite en aerosol

1 pizca de sal

Queso de canasta rallado al gusto

1 aguacate en rebanadas

3 jitomates picados en cubos

½ kilo de cebolla picada

Hojas de cilantro

Pimienta negra al gusto

Salsa:

3 tomates verdes, en cubos

3 cucharadas de hojas de cilantro

Pimienta negra al gusto

Sal al gusto

Agua, la necesaria

Chiles serranos al gusto

1 rábano picado

Preparación:

Rociar la parrilla en frío con aceite en aerosol. Encender la parrilla.

Mezclar los ingredientes de la marinada. Agregar el pollo y reservar.

Poner a asar primero los nopales con el ajo y después el pollo con un poco más de aceite en aerosol y agregar una pizca de sal; voltearlas para cocer.

Cortar el pollo en cubos medianos. Servir sobre el nopal, agregar el queso, aguacate, jitomate, cebolla, cilantro y pimienta.

Salsa:

Licuar los tomates, sal, pimienta, cilantro y chiles serranos.

Servir la salsa cruda sobre los huaraches de nopal.

Fajitas de res con nopales

Ingredientes:

2 nopales del tamaño de la palma de una mano

100 gramos de bistec de res sin grasa

¼ de cebolla

1 diente de ajo

1 chile serrano o jalapeño

Sal y pimienta al gusto

Limón

Salsa inglesa

Preparación:

Picar el ajo muy finamente. En un refractario colocar la carne cortada en tiras, con el ajo, sal y pimienta, el jugo de medio limón, la salsa inglesa y el chile cortado en delgadas rajas. Dejar marinar por dos horas en el refrigerador.

Cortar la cebolla y los nopales en tiras y poner a asar en una sartén de teflón; cuando los nopales empiecen a cambiar de color agregar la carne junto con la marinada, dejar cocinar hasta que la carne y los nopales estén bien cocidos.

Se recomienda acompañar con un jitomate cortado en cubos sazonado con sal y limón.

Nopales con huevo

Ingredientes:

½ kilo de nopales picados y cocidos

2 jitomates medianos picados

1 cebolla chica picada

2 chiles verdes picados

4 huevos

Aceite

Sal

Preparación:

En una cacerola se pone aceite a calentar y enseguida se le agrega el jitomate, cebolla y el chile verde a que se sofrían, después se agregan los nopales y por último se le agregan los huevos y la sal, se mueven constantemente para que no se peguen.

Nopales a la vinagreta

Ingredientes:

6 nopales en tiras

2 cucharadas de vinagre de manzana

Queso de hebra en tiras o fresco en cuadritos

Cebolla en rodajas al gusto

Chile jalapeño en tiras

4 cucharadas de aceite de oliva

Trocitos de papa hervidos

Sal

Preparación:

Para que no quede muy baboso el nopal se hierve con sal y un limón exprimido. Por otro lado en un sartén poner el aceite de oliva y agregar el chile, luego la cebolla hasta que queden transparentes; se agregan los nopales y se fríen un momento, después se le añade una pizca de sal y el vinagre y se deja en hervor un rato, por último se le incorporan el queso y la papa.

Papas con nopales

Ingredientes:

4 papas grandes

4 nopales

1 taza de tomates verdes

Sal al gusto

1 taza de agua

2 chiles verdes o un pimiento verde

Preparación:

Primero hay que asar los nopales, limpiarlos bajo un chorro de agua y cortarlos en tiras. Posteriormente cortamos las papas en cubos y luego los colocamos en una sartén o cacerola agregando media taza de agua.

El resto de los ingredientes se licuan junto con los chiles y el tomate verde. Luego se incorpora todo: las papas y los nopales junto con una pizca de sal y se deja cocinar por diez minutos o hasta que estén cocidas las papas.

Se acompaña con arroz.

Tortitas de camarones con nopales

Ingredientes:

2 tazas de nopalitos tiernos cortados en tiritas

2 chiles guajillo cocidos, sin semillas

2 chiles anchos cocidos, sin semillas

1 jitomate cocido

1 diente de ajo

1 ramito pequeño de cilantro fresco

½ cebolla mediana rebanada

Consomé de camarón al gusto

1 taza de camarón seco

½ taza de pan molido

3 huevos, separadas yemas y claras

Aceite para freír

Preparación:

Se baten las claras a punto de turrón. Se agregan una a una las yemas y se mezclan con cuidado.

Se va poniendo el camarón con el pan por cucharaditas espolvoreándolo y revolviendo la mezcla con cuidado para que el huevo no se baje.

Probar la mezcla, si está muy salada agregar pan molido. Se pone aceite suficiente en un sartén caliente y se van agregando cucharadas soperas de la mezcla para que se formen las tortitas; bajar un poco la flama, se doran rápido. Con una palita, ir volteándolas, para que se doren parejito. Sacar y poner en toallitas de papel a que escurran. Moler los chiles, jitomate y ajo.

Rebanar la cebolla y freír a que acitrone, escurrir el exceso de grasa y agregar la salsa colada. Poner agua o caldo. Colocar los nopalitos escurridos, el cilantro y agregar las tortitas. Tapar y dejar hervir unos minutos.

Si falta sal, agregar un poco de consomé, revolver y servir con tortillas calientes. Este plato se acompaña antes con una crema de fríjol.

Nopales empanizados con queso

Ingredientes:

180 gramos de queso Oaxaca deshebrado

1 huevo

Arroz blanco preparado

¾ de taza de pan molido

6 nopales grandes cocidos enteros

3 jitomates medianos

¼ de cebolla

1 diente de ajo

½ taza de aceite para freír

Sal y pimienta al gusto

Preparación:

Los nopales cocidos se abren por un costado a lo largo, procurando no abrir el otro extremo, formando un saquito. Se rellenan con el queso y se cierran ensartándoles un palillo en posición vertical.

El huevo se bate y se condimenta con sal y pimienta; se pasan los nopales por el huevo y luego por el pan molido hasta cubrirlos totalmente.

Se fríen en el aceite bien caliente y se escurren sobre una servilleta de papel para quitar el exceso de grasa

Se prepara un caldillo licuando los jitomates con el ajo y la cebolla.

Se sofríen en la salsa en una cucharada de aceite y se sazona con sal y pimienta.

Se sirven sobre una cama de arroz y se bañan con el caldillo.

Tacos de nopales

Ingredientes:

12 nopales picados

18 tortillas

1 cebolla picada

1 manojo de cilantro picado

¼ taza de aceite de oliva

6 dientes de ajo

1 cucharadita de orégano

Sal

Preparación:

Poner a cocer en agua hirviendo con un pedazo de cebolla los nopales hasta que estén tiernos. Ya que estén cocidos enjuagar con agua fría y escurrir perfectamente. En una sartén poner a calentar el aceite de oliva y acitronar la cebolla junto con el ajo, enseguida agregar el cilantro picado y finalmente los nopales sazonando

con sal. Una vez fritos se les incorpora el orégano espol-
voreando y se procede a hacer los tacos. Se pueden servir
fríos o calientes.

Nopales rellenos con queso

Ingredientes:

10 nopales

300 gramos de queso fresco

2 huevos

½ taza de harina de trigo

½ kilo de tomate

2 chiles serrano

¼ de cebolla

5 cucharadas de aceite

Ajo a su gusto

Epazote a su gusto

Sal

Preparación:

Lave y cueza los nopales en poca agua, agréguele
sal al primer hervor y después escúrralos.

Quítele la cáscara y lave los tomates, enseguida
licuelos con los chiles serranos la cebolla y el ajo.

Lave el epazote y coloque en un nopal, una rebanada de queso y una hoja de epazote, cúbralo con otro
nopal y asegúrelos con palillos.

Enharine los nopales, bata las claras a punto de turrón, añádale las yemas y la harina mezclando en forma
envolvente.

Pase los nopales por el huevo batido y fríalos.
Aparte fría la salsa y agregue agua, sazónela con sal y deje hervir.
Sirva los nopales acompañados con la salsa.

Nopales con chorizo

Ingredientes:

10 nopales cocidos y cortados en cuadros

2 cebollas medianas en rebanadas finas

2 ajos picados finamente

½ kilo de longaniza o chorizo

Aceite

Preparación:

En una sartén con aceite se fríe el chorizo, cuando esté cocido se le agrega la cebolla, cuando ésta se cueza se le agrega el ajo. Se le agregan los nopales y se dejan cocinando por unos diez minutos.

Nopales enchilados con pollo

Ingredientes:

6 nopales

1 cebolla asada (para molerla)

1 trozo de cebolla para cocer el nopal

3 dientes de ajo

2 kilos de pollo en trozos

3 jitomates asados y pelados

3 chiles guajillos

3 chiles pasilla asados

3 xoconostles pelados y picados

2 cucharadas de sal y dos de pimienta

Preparación:

Corte los nopales en rajitas y cuézalos en agua con sal, cebolla y escurra.

Por separado fría el pollo, sal y pimienta.

Muela el jitomate con la cebolla, el ajo restante y los chiles guajillo y pasilla, agregue a la carne y deje cocer todo; rectifique la sal, añada los xoconostles partidos en cuadritos y los nopales, y deje hervir unos minutos más para que todo esté sazonado.

Nopales especiales

Ingredientes:

½ kilo de nopales picados y cocidos

½ kilo de papas cocidas y picadas

2 jitomates picados (sin piel y sin semillas)

1 cebolla grande fileteada y macerada

3 aguacates cortados en tiras

1 latita de chiles en vinagre

1 taza de salsa vinagreta

200 gramos de jamón cortado en tiras

1 ramita de cilantro picada

Tostadas de maíz

Preparación:

En una ensaladera mezcle todos los ingredientes con la salsa vinagreta (con excepción de las tostadas) dejando reposar durante unos minutos para que tome sabor.

Sirva sobre las tostadas adornando con un poco de lechuga tierna.

Pollo con nopales

Ingredientes:

10 nopales chicos, tiernos y limpios

1 pollo en piezas y limpio

5 chiles poblanos asados y desvenados

1 diente de ajo

1 cebolla

Aceite, el necesario

Preparación:

Acomode el pollo en una cacerola, salpimente a su gusto y dórelo con su propia grasa; si no suelta mucha agregue un poco de aceite.

Una vez que se haya dorado un poco, añada los nopales y los chiles en rajas a que se frían con el pollo, moviendo para que no se queme.

Muela el ajo, la cebolla y los chiles restantes con un poco de agua; esta salsa añádala al pollo frito y deje que hierva un poco, rectifique la sazón.

Si le queda muy espeso agregue un poco de agua y vuelva a rectificar la sazón.

Mixiotes de nopales con pollo

Ingredientes:

½ kilo de nopalitos limpios y cocidos

½ cabeza de ajo limpio y picado

½ pollo en piezas

1 cebolla grande en rodajas

3 xoconostles pelados y picados

2 ramitas de epazote picado

50 gramos de manteca o aceite

12 hojas de mixiote e hilo para amarrar

1 taza de agua o caldo

Chile morita tostado y molido

Sal al gusto

Preparación:

Muela el chile en media taza de agua, en una cacerola coloque los ingredientes (menos las hojas y el pollo) y revuelva con sal y chile.

Deje remojando ahí las piezas de pollo por espacio de dos horas, en un trozo de hoja para mixiote, coloque una pieza de pollo y agregue un poco de los demás ingredientes, amarre y ponga a cocer en una vaporera a fuego lento por cincuenta minutos aproximadamente.

Chicharrón con nopales

Ingredientes:

4 nopales cocidos rebanados

6 tomates sin cáscara y asados

8 chiles pasilla asados

1 jitomate asado

1 diente de ajo

½ cebolla

1 taza de agua

2 cucharadas de aceite

100 gramos de chicharrón delgado

Sal al gusto

Preparación:

Muela los tomates, chiles, jitomate, ajo, cebolla, sal, agua y vacíe en una cacerola.

Fría en el aceite y deje en el fuego hasta que espese.

Enseguida agregue el chicharrón; los nopales déjelos dar un hervor para que todo se sazone: sirva caliente.

Nopales en su penca

Ingredientes:

1 penca de nopal o nopal grande

½ kilo de nopales

¼ kilo de chorizo o longaniza

1 cebolla

¼ queso asadero o Oaxaca

Pimienta al gusto

Sal al gusto

1 cordón o hilo

Preparación:

Abrir el nopal grande por la parte de abajo, y con la mano, separarlo de sus paredes hasta dejarlo estilo bolsa. Aparte cortar los nopales en cubitos y picar la cebolla en cuadros pequeños.

Freír aparte los nopales con el chorizo, cebolla, sal y pimienta. Agregar el queso al final hasta que se funda

Rellenar la bolsa de nopal y cerrarla con el hilo.

Poner directo a las brasas en un asador de leña o una fogata hasta que se cueza el nopal grande.

Huarache de nopal con champiñones

Ingredientes:

2 nopales asados

1 taza de champiñones cocidos con epazote

½ taza de queso manchego rallado

Para la salsa:

¼ de cebolla asada

Chile de árbol al gusto

2 jitomates asados

Preparación:

Licuar los ingredientes de la salsa. Colocar los champiñones, el queso y la salsa encima del nopal. Gratinar en el horno a 150° C.

Nopal con huevo estrellado

Ingredientes:

4 nopales asados

4 huevos estrellados

1 taza de frijoles con caldo

1 cucharadita de caldo de chile chipotle

Aceite en aerosol

Preparación:

Licuar los frijoles con el caldo del chile chipotle. Freír los huevos de dos en dos. Colocar los huevos sobre los nopales y verter encima la salsa de frijol y chipotle.

Crepas de nopal y queso

Ingredientes:

Para hacer las crepas:

5 huevos

1 cucharadita de sal

1 taza de harina integral

½ taza de leche

4 cucharadas de mantequilla derretida

Para hacer el relleno:

½ taza de mantequilla

2 dientes de ajo, machacado

1 cebolla picada

8 nopales cocidos, cortados en cuadritos

½ kilo de queso manchego, rallado

Sal y pimienta al gusto

Preparación:

Para las crepas, licuar los ingredientes. Dejar reposar treinta minutos. Calentar una sartén redonda, engrasar con un poco de mantequilla, colocar un cucharón de la masa e inclinar para que se llene toda la sartén; cuando empiece a dorar la orilla voltear. Seguir la misma operación con el resto de la masa. Guardar las crepas envueltas en un trapo limpio.

Para hacer el relleno derretir la mantequilla en una sartén, agregar el ajo y la cebolla hasta que se acitronen.

Agregar los nopales y sazonar con sal y pimienta, y por último, añadir el queso manchego.

Rellenar las crepas. Servir acompañado de una deliciosa salsa verde.

Nopales con queso y epazote

Ingredientes:

8 nopales tiernitos

1 manojo de epazote, lavado (sólo las hojas)

2 chiles cuaresmeños, cortados en rajas

Aceite de oliva

1 taza de queso Oaxaca, deshebrado

Sal

Preparación:

Limpiar los nopales, cortar la parte más gruesa del tallo y de ese mismo lado hacer cortes, esto sirve para que se cuezan más rápido.

Calentar un comal grueso y untarle un poco de aceite de oliva, colocar los nopales encima, sazonar con sal, darles la vuelta después de cinco minutos y sobre los nopales colocar el queso Oaxaca; añadir unas hojitas de epazote y unas rajas de chile cuaresmeño sobre los nopales.

Bajar el fuego y retirar de la lumbre hasta que el queso se haya derretido. Servir de inmediato. Estos nopalitos pueden servir como botanita o bien como plato fuerte si se sirven acompañados de arroz.

Tortitas mexicanas

Ingredientes:

5 nopales cocidos y picados

150 gramos de queso Oaxaca deshebrado

½ taza de harina

2 huevos (separadas las claras de las yemas)

Pizca de sal

Aceite vegetal

Preparación:

En un recipiente revolver los nopales con el queso, la harina y la sal.

Batir las claras a punto de turrón y agregar las yemas una por una; cuando estén integradas, añadir la preparación de nopales con movimiento envolvente.

Tomar unas cucharadas de la mezcla y freírlas en una sartén con aceite hasta que comiencen a dorar; retirar las tortitas y ponerlas sobre papel absorbente para quitarles el exceso de grasa.

Al servir las tortitas, se pueden acompañar con lechuga, guarnición de brócoli o la verdura que se prefiera.

Nopales a la mexicana

Ingredientes:

4 nopales medianos

3 jitomates finamente picados

4 tomates verdes picados

1 manojo de cebollitas cambray

2 dientes de ajo picados

2 chiles verdes picados

Aceite vegetal

Una pizca de sal

Preparación:

Cocer los nopales en agua suficiente para cubrirlos; posteriormente escurrirlos.

Sofreír los jitomates, los tomates, las cebollitas, los ajos y los chiles hasta que los tomates estén cocidos. Integrar los nopales y sazonar con sal. Cocinar hasta que se calienten y retirar del fuego.

Tamales de nopal con huevo

Ingredientes:

500 gramos de manteca de cerdo

1 cucharada de sal

1 kilo de harina para tamales

1 cucharadita de polvo para hornear

1½ taza de caldo de pollo o el necesario

½ paquete de hojas para tamales, remojadas

Del relleno:

½ cebolla chica finamente picada

6 nopales picados, cocidos y escurridos

5 huevos revueltos

Sal al gusto

Preparación:

Bata la manteca de cerdo hasta que esté blanca y esponjada, agregue la sal y la harina poco a poco (previamente mezclada con el polvo para hornear), añada el caldo de pollo y mezcle hasta obtener una pasta suave y esponjosa. Ponga una bolita de masa en un vaso con agua, si flota ya está lista.

Saltee la cebolla, cuando esté transparente agregue los nopales, mezcle perfectamente, vierta los huevos y sal al gusto, mezcle hasta que cuezan, verifique el sabor y reserve.

Coloque dos cucharadas de masa en una hoja para tamal, extiéndala ligeramente, ponga un poco de relleno y envuelva, haga lo mismo con el resto de la masa. Cuézalos al vapor durante una hora o veinte minutos en olla de presión.

Nopales asados

Ingredientes:

Nopales enteros (de preferencia chicos)

Queso en rebanadas muy delgadas

Preparación:

Se colocan los nopales enteros sobre un comal o sobre la parrilla donde se asa la carne y se dejan con fuego lento hasta que se cueza. Se les pueden poner unas rebanaditas de queso arriba antes de servirlos.

Los nopales asados son comida muy rica para los días de campo, como botana o para acompañar la carne asada.

Atún con nopales

Ingredientes:

500 gramos de atún ahumado cortado en rodajas

1 ramito de hierbas de olor

1 cebolla grande

5 jitomates grandes maduros

2 dientes de ajo

1 limón (su jugo)

Aceite para freír

4 nopales picados en juliana y cocidos

10 aceitunas negras deshuesadas

Sal al gusto

Pimienta al gusto

Preparación:

En una cazuela poner aceite a calentar, añadir la cebolla picada, los nopales y los jitomates pelados y sin semillas, así como lás hierbas de olor. Sofreír a fuego lento, durante diez minutos, agregar el atún y el ajo picado. Salpimentar y cocer veinte minutos más a fuego lento. Cinco minutos antes de terminar la cocción añadir el jugo de limón y las aceitunas deshuesadas.

Encurtido de nopales

Ingredientes:

18 nopales pequeños

1 manojo de cebollitas de cambray

5 dientes de ajo

1 cucharada de pimienta gorda

2 chiles de árbol secos

1 cucharada de bicarbonato de sodio

½ de taza de aceite de oliva

½ taza de vinagre blanco

Sal al gusto

Preparación:

En una sartén calentar el aceite, sofreír los nopales y las cebollitas (sin rabo), agregar los ajos, la pimienta; los chiles y sal, mover para evitar que se peguen.

Aparte combinar el vinagre con dos tazas de agua y reservar.

Espolvorear el bicarbonato sobre los nopales, verter el agua con el vinagre y cocinar hasta que hierva (mover constantemente); retirar del fuego, dejar enfriar y servir.

Nopales con chile piquín

Ingredientes:

> 2 tazas de nopales frescos en tiras sin espinas
>
> 1 cucharadita de aceite de oliva
>
> ½ taza de cebolla
>
> ½ cucharadita de chile piquín

Preparación:

Ponga los nopales en un sartén y cubra con agua. Deje hervir durante veinte minutos.

Escurra el agua de los nopales y enjuague bien.

Caliente el aceite en un sartén.

Sofría las cebollas en el aceite caliente.

Agregue los nopales cocidos y el chile piquín. Cocine hasta que estén bien calientes.

Frijoles con nopales

Ingredientes:

> 250 gramos de frijoles canario, remojados
>
> 4 chiles guajillos asados, remojados y licuados
>
> 1 chipotle de lata, molido con el guajillo

3 jitomates asados, pelados y picados

4 cucharadas de cebolla finamente picada

3 cucharadas de aceite

6 nopales cosidos cortados en tiras

1 rama de epazote

Sal

Preparación:

Cocer los frijoles en agua fresca, hasta que estén suaves, aproximadamente hora y media. Ponerles sal y licuarlos con su caldo.

En el aceite freír la cebolla, añadir los tomates picados, revolver bien y agregar los chiles molidos, dejar cocinar diez minutos a fuego lento y agregar los frijoles molidos, epazote y los nopales. Esperar a que todo tome sabor y servir caliente.

Enchiladas de nopal

Ingredientes:

600 gramos nopales cocidos y en cubos

200 mililitros de crema

400 gramos lechuga

200 gramos queso panela rallado

600 mililitros agua

30 tortillas de maíz

400 gramos pasta de chile pasilla

12 gramos caldo de pollo

Preparación:

Calentar las tortillas y rellenarlas con los nopales.

Calentar la pasta de chile pasilla con el caldo de pollo y agua.

Cocinar por diez minutos; sazonar al gusto.

En un plato colocar las enchiladas, bañarlas con salsa y acompañarlas con lechuga, la crema y el queso.

Charales pobres

Ingredientes:

6 nopales cocidos y picados

½ tazas de charales

3 papas medianas (cocidas y peladas)

1 diente de ajo

¼ de tomate verde

4 chiles verdes

½ cebolla

1 ramita de cilantro

Aceite, el necesario

Sal al gusto

Preparación:

Se hierven los tomates con los chiles verdes, se licuan con la cebolla, ajo, cilantro y la sal.

Se doran los charales en aceite, una vez dorados se quita un poco de aceite a la sartén y se agrega la salsa; cuando hierve, se añade una taza de agua, las papas y los nopales cocidos y picados, se tapa y se deja cocer a fuego lento durante diez minutos o hasta que se ablanden los charales.

Se sirve caliente.

Pulpos y nopalitos en escabeche

Ingredientes:

6 nopalitos en tiritas

1 kilo de pulpo

1 pizca de bicarbonato

1 cebolla rebanada

1 cucharada de orégano

¾ de taza de vinagre de manzana

½ taza de aceite de oliva

Sal, pimienta y azúcar

Chiles en vinagre al gusto

1 manojo de rabanitos (para adornar)

Preparación:

Se cuece el pulpo en agua hirviendo de cuarenta a sesenta minutos, según el tamaño, y se rebana delgado.

Luego, se cuecen los nopalitos en agua hirviendo con una pizca de bicarbonato.

Finalmente se revuelve con el resto de los ingredientes, aligerando un poco con agua y se adorna con los rabanitos.

Postres y panes

Mermelada de nopales

Ingredientes:

½ kilo de nopales

2 tazas de azúcar

2 manzanas (cáscara y los corazones)

1 taza de agua

1 cucharada sopera de jugo de limón

1 pizca de bicarbonato

Utensilios:

Cacerola con capacidad de 1 litro

Cuchillo de acero inoxidable

Pala de madera

Frascos de vidrio limpios

Etiqueta adhesiva

Licuadora

Preparación:

Se pone a hervir el agua con las cáscaras y los corazones de manzana.

Se lavan muy bien los nopales, se pican y se licuan con el agua en donde se cocieron las cáscaras y corazones de manzana.

Se vacía en una cacerola, se agrega el azúcar y se coloca a fuego medio de cinco a diez minutos.

Al momento de hervir se agrega el jugo de limón y la pizca de bicarbonato de sodio.

La espuma formada se va retirando y se agita constantemente con la pala de madera para evitar que se pegue. Cuando deje de hacer espuma y al mover se vea el fondo del recipiente, la mermelada estará lista.

A continuación se envasa en caliente en frascos de vidrio previamente esterilizados, se deja un espacio de un centímetro entre el producto y la tapa, apretando perfectamente para provocar vacío.

Etiquete indicando el nombre del producto, fecha de elaboración y de caducidad.

Duración: La mermelada de nopal elaborada de esta forma tiene una duración aproximada de tres meses.

Recomendaciones: Se guarda en lugar fresco seco y oscuro.

Una vez abierto el producto, es necesario mantenerlo en refrigeración.

Pay de nopal

Ingredientes:

250 gramos de mermelada de nopal

300 gramos de harina

1 barrita de mantequilla

75 gramos de azúcar

4 huevos

1 cucharadita de polvo para hornear

Preparación:

La harina se cierne con el polvo de hornear, se mezcla con la mantequilla, se forma una fuente y en el centro se agregan tres huevos; se bate hasta formar una masa suave.

Se forman dos porciones iguales, se extiende la primera porción en un molde previamente engrasado y enharinado, se rellena con la mermelada y con la otra porción se cubre el molde, se bate el otro huevo, se baña con la brocha y se le espolvorea el azúcar.

Se cuece en el horno por espacio de treinta minutos a 250° centígrados o hasta que al introducir un palillo en el pay salga limpio.

Pastel de nopal

Ingredientes:

375 gramos de mermelada de nopal

1 kilo de mantequilla

1 kilo de harina

1 kilo de huevo

4 cucharadas de polvo para hornear

Preparación:

Derrita la mantequilla, agregue la harina cernida con el polvo de hornear. Sin dejar de batir, agregue los huevos de uno en uno, sólo agregue las yemas y la mermelada, al final agregue a la pasta las claras a punto de turrón en forma envolvente; vacíe en un molde grande, engrasado y enharinado.

Cueza unos veinte minutos en horno precalentado a fuego medio, o hasta que al introducir un palillo de madera en el pastel, salga seco. Saque el pastel del molde. Déjelo enfriar antes de adornarlo.

Empanadas de nopal

Ingredientes:

1½ kilo de nopalitos cocidos y picados

1 kilo de harina

350 gramos de azúcar

350 gramos de mantequilla

¾ de kilo de huevo

250 gramos de levadura

Preparación:

Con la harina cernida se hace una fuente y se incorporan los ingredientes, el azúcar, la levadura, la mantequilla y el huevo, se bate hasta hacer una pasta tersa, se deja reposar media hora.

Se hacen las empanadas rellenas con los nopalitos y se meten al horno durante treinta minutos, a 250° centígrados.

Gelatina de nopal

Ingredientes:

1 litro de agua de nopal

30 gramos de grenetina

1 taza de azúcar

½ litro de agua

Preparación:

Se hierve medio litro de agua con azúcar, se hidrata la grenetina con agua fría.

Se mezcla la grenetina hidratada con el agua hirviendo y se deja enfriar, se agrega el agua de nopal y se mete al refrigerador a que cuaje.

Dulce de nopal

Ingredientes:

2 nopales (cocidos sin sal)

1 lata de leche condensada

2 cucharadas de azúcar

2 sobrecitos de grenetina

½ taza de agua fría

Preparación:

Licue los nopales con la leche y el azúcar, cuele. Aparte disuelva la grenetina en media taza de agua fría, debe disolverla en baño María.

Mezcle la grenetina con los nopales, distribuya en dulceras y refrigere hasta la hora de servir.

Galletas de nopal

Ingredientes:

1 lata de leche condensada

1 taza de nopales cocidos en cuadritos

1 taza de avena

1 taza de harina integral, cernida

1 cucharada de polvo para hornear

1 cucharadita de anís molido

½ cucharadita de canela en polvo

1 cucharadita de vainilla

Preparación:

Se precalienta el horno a 200° centígrados.

Se licua la leche condensada con los nopales. Esta mezcla se vierte en un recipiente y se añade el resto de los ingredientes.

Mezclar e integrar.

En charolas engrasadas y enharinadas se ponen porciones de la mezcla formando las galletas.

Hornear por veinte minutos o hasta que doren.

Sacar del horno y dejar enfriar por completo.

Índice

Esta edición se imprimió en   Mayo de 2011   Impre Imagen
José María Morelos y Pavón Mz 5 Lt 1 Ecatepec.Edo de México
El Tiraje fue de 1000 Ejemplares.

Lovable CHARACTER CAKES

Debbie Brown

Lovable CHARACTER CAKES

Debbie Brown

MEREHURST

DEDICATION

To my dear Nan, Eliza Lewis, who knew that love is the greatest gift. Her gift to me is treasured.

First published 1999 by Merehurst Ltd
Ferry House, 51–57 Lacy Road,
Putney, London SW15 1PR
Copyright © Debra Brown 1999
Debra Brown has asserted her right under
the Copyright, Designs and Patents Act,
1988
ISBN 1-85391-727-3
Reprinted in 2000

Editor: Helen Southall
Design: Anita Ruddell
Photography by Clive Streeter
Colour separation by Bright Arts,
Hong Kong
Printed in Singapore by Tien Wah Press

Pages 14–18 **FIREMAN SAM**™
© 1985 Prism Art & Design Ltd
manufactured 1999. Based on the
Television Series Fireman Sam
produced by Bumper Films for S4C
Licensed by BBC Worldwide Ltd

Pages 19–23 **THE FLOWER FAIRIES**™
Copyright © The Estate of Cicely Mary
Barker, 1999. The Candytuft Fairy
illustration (page 19) from FLOWER
FAIRIES OF THE GARDEN Copyright ©
The Estate of Cicely Mary Barker, 1944,
1990. Reproduced by kind permission of
Frederick Warne & Co

Pages 24–27 **THE WOMBLES**™
© Elisabeth Beresford/FilmFair Ltd 1999
Licensed by Copyrights

Pages 28–31 **MY LITTLE PONY**™
© 1999 Hasbro International Inc.
Licensed by 3D Licensing Ltd.

Pages 32–35
DENNIS & GNASHER™
Dennis & Gnasher is a trade mark of
D.C. Thomson & Co. Ltd.
© D.C. Thomson & Co. Ltd. 1999

Pages 36–39 **KIPPER**™
© Mick Inkpen 1999
Books published by Hodder & Stoughton
Licensed by Copyrights

Pages 40–42 **GARFIELD**
© 1999 PAWS INCORPORATED.
ALL RIGHTS RESERVED.

MR.MEN   LITTLE MISS

Pages 43–46 **LITTLE MISS**™
MR. MEN and LITTLE MISS™
© 1999 Mrs. Roger Hargreaves
By permission of Price Stern & Sloan, Inc.,
a division of Penguin Putnam Inc.

Pages 47–50
SONIC™ **THE HEDGEHOG**
Sega, Sonic The Hedgehog and all
related characters and indicia are
trademarks of SEGA.
© SEGA ENTERPRISES LTD. 1991/1992

Pages 51–55 **BRAMBLY HEDGE**™
© Jill Barklem 1999
Books published by Harper Collins
Licensed by Copyrights

Pages 56–59
BANANAS IN PYJAMAS™
Produced by Merehurst Limited under
licence from the Australian Broadcasting
Corporation.
© Australian Broadcasting Corporation
1999.
Original song by Carey Blyton.

Pages 60–63 **SUPER MARIO**™
™ & © 1999 NINTENDO.
All rights reserved.

Pages 64–68 and 69–71
WALLACE & GROMIT™
Wallace & Gromit [Word Mark] is a
trademark of Aardman/Wallace & Gromit
Limited and is used under licence.
© Aardman/Wallace & Gromit Limited
1989. Licensed by BBC Worldwide Limited

Pages 72–76 **RUGRATS**®
© 1999 Viacom International Inc.
All Rights Reserved.
Created by Klasky Csupo Inc.

Pages 77–79 **RUPERT**™
Rupert characters ™ & © Express
Newspapers p.l.c.
Licensed by Nelvana Marketing Inc.
NELVANA is a registered trademark of
Nelvana Limited
UK Representative Copyright Promotions

Pages 80–83 **BABAR**™
Babar Characters ™ & ©
Laurent de Brunhoff.

Pages 84–87 **SESAME STREET**™
© 1999 CTW. Sesame Street Muppets
© 1999 The Jim Henson Company.
All rights reserved. Sesame Street and the
Sesame Street sign are trademarks of
CTW. Licensed with TLC.

Pages 88–90 **BARNEY**™
© 1999 Lyons Partnership, L.P.
All rights reserved.
The character and name Barney and the
overlapping dino spots, and the Barney
and star logos are trademarks of Lyons
Partnership, L.P.
Barney and the Barney and star logo are
Reg. U.S. Pat. & Tm. Off.

Contents

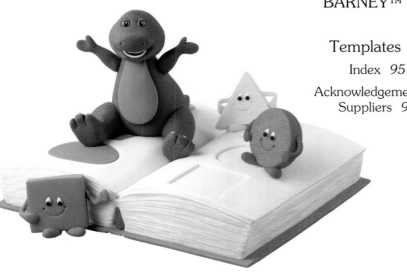

Introduction

Following the phenomenal success of *Favourite Character Cakes*, shown on page 96, I felt that a collection of lovable characters would be just as popular and a big hit with children and adults alike.

Many people want to see their own particular favourite character and when *Favourite Character Cakes* was published I was often asked 'But where is Rupert?', or 'How could you leave out Sesame Street?' Hopefully, this new collection of cakes will fill the gap.

From timeless Rupert Bear, the delightful Flower Fairies and lovable Barney, to gorgeously cute Kipper, there is a character for everyone, including cakes for the young at heart who remember their own favourites the first time round.

Children just adore the characters they see everywhere around them. They become their friends in toys, videos and books. Many will not go to bed without their favourite character toy to cuddle up to at bedtime.

Of course, the bright colours associated with many characters appeal to children. Some cakes in this book have been painted on the surface, to cut down on food colouring content, but remember, their special day comes but once a year.

A birthday cake themed on a favourite lovable character will make someone's birthday a special memory, forever.

7

Basic Recipes & Techniques

These simple recipes are suitable for making any of the cakes in this book. Together with the helpful section on Techniques that follows, they will guarantee good results.

Basic Recipes

MADEIRA SPONGE CAKE

The secret of successful novelty cake-making is to start with a firm, moist cake that can be cut and shaped without crumbling. A Madeira recipe is a good choice and can be flavoured to give variety.

To make a Madeira cake suitable for any of the designs in this book, first grease and line the required bakeware (see the chart on pages 12–13), then follow the steps below. For ingredients, see pages 12–13.

1 Preheat the oven to 160°C (325°F) Gas 3. Sift the two types of flour together into a bowl.

2 Put the soft margarine and caster (superfine) sugar together in a large mixing bowl, and beat until the mixture is pale and fluffy.

3 Gradually add the eggs, one at a time, with a spoonful of the flour, beating well after each addition. Beat in any flavouring required (see right).

4 Fold the remaining flour into the mixture.

5 Spoon the mixture into the bakeware. Make a dip in the top with the back of the spoon.

6 Bake in the centre of the oven until a skewer inserted in the centre comes out clean (see chart for approximate time).

7 Leave to cool for 5 minutes, then turn out on to a wire rack and leave to cool completely. When cold, store in an airtight container until ready to use.

Flavourings

Vanilla Add 1 teaspoon vanilla essence to *every 6-egg mixture*.
Lemon Add the grated rind and/or juice of 1 lemon to *every 6-egg mixture*.
Chocolate Add 2–3 tablespoons unsweetened cocoa powder mixed with 1 tablespoon milk to *every 6-egg mixture*.
Almond Add 1 teaspoon almond essence and 2–3 tablespoons ground almonds to *every 6-egg mixture*.

SUGARPASTE

For convenience, I recommend using ready-made sugarpaste (rolled fondant), which is of high quality and easily available from cake decorating suppliers and supermarkets. However, if you prefer to make your own, use this simple recipe.

Makes 625g (1¼ lb)
1 egg white
2 tablespoons liquid glucose
625g (1¼ lb) icing (confectioners') sugar
a little white vegetable fat (shortening), if required

1 Put the egg white and liquid glucose into a bowl.

2 Sift the icing sugar into the bowl, a little at a time, stirring until the mixture thickens.

3 Turn out on to a surface dusted with icing sugar and knead the paste until smooth and pliable. If the paste is a little dry and cracked, knead in a little white fat.

4 Put immediately into a polythene bag, or wrap in cling film (plastic wrap), and store in an airtight container.

BUTTERCREAM

As well as making a delicious filling between layers of cake, a thin coat of buttercream spread all over the cake fills any small gaps and provides a smooth surface on which to apply the sugarpaste (rolled fondant). Buttercream can also be flavoured.

Makes about 500g (1lb)
125g (4oz/½ cup) butter, softened, or soft margarine
1 tablespoon milk
375g (12oz/2½ cups) icing (confectioners') sugar, sifted

1 Put the butter or soft margarine in a bowl.

2 Add the milk and/or any flavouring (see below).

3 Sift the icing sugar into the bowl, a little at a time, beating well after each addition, until all the sugar is incorporated and the buttercream has a light, creamy texture.

4 Store the buttercream in an airtight container until required.

Flavourings

Vanilla Add 1 teaspoon vanilla essence.
Lemon Replace the milk with fresh or concentrated lemon juice.
Chocolate Mix the milk and 2 tablespoons unsweetened cocoa powder to a paste and add to the mixture.
Coffee Mix the milk and 1 tablespoon instant coffee powder to a paste and add to the mixture.

ROYAL ICING

Makes about 280g (9oz)
1 egg white
250–280g (8–9oz/1¾ cups) icing
(confectioners') sugar, sifted

1 Put the egg white in a bowl. Beat in the icing sugar, a little at a time, until the icing is firm and glossy, and forms peaks when the spoon is pulled out.

2 Cover the bowl with a damp cloth for a few minutes before use.

PASTILLAGE

When pastillage icing is rolled out and left to dry, it dries so hard it 'snaps' when broken. It will not bend or lose its shape when dry and resists moisture, although extremely damp conditions will affect it.

When using pastillage, you have to work quite quickly as it forms a crust soon after being exposed to the air. It is therefore unsuitable for modelling unless you mix it 50/50 with sugarpaste (rolled fondant).

Pastillage can be obtained in high-quality powder form from cake decorating suppliers, but this recipe is very simple.

Makes about 375g (12oz)
1 egg white
345g (11oz/2¼ cups) icing
(confectioners') sugar, sifted
2 teaspoons gum tragacanth (see page 10)

1 Put the egg white in a bowl and add 280g (9oz) icing sugar a little at a time, mixing well after each addition.

2 Sprinkle the gum tragacanth over the top and put aside for about 10 minutes.

3 Turn the mixture out on to a surface and knead in the remaining icing sugar.

4 Double wrap in polythene or cling film (plastic wrap) and store in an airtight container until required.

PETAL PASTE

Petal (or flower) paste produces very fine results and, as its name suggests, is ideal for making flowers and leaves, such as those on the Flower Fairies cake, for example. It can be bought ready-made from cake decorating suppliers (either direct or by mail order), or you can make your own as follows.

Makes about 500g (1lb)
5 teaspoons cold water
2 teaspoons powdered gelatine
500g (1lb/3 cups) icing (confectioners')
sugar, sifted
3 teaspoons gum tragacanth (see page 10)
2 teaspoons liquid glucose
3 teaspoons white vegetable fat (shortening)
1 medium egg white

1 Mix the water and gelatine together in a small heatproof bowl and leave to stand for 30 minutes. Sift the icing sugar and gum tragacanth into the bowl of an electric mixer and fit the bowl to the machine.

2 Place the bowl with the gelatine mixture over a saucepan of hot water and stir until the gelatine has dissolved. Warm a teaspoon in hot water, then measure out the liquid glucose (the heat should help ease the glucose off the spoon). Add the glucose and white fat to the gelatine mixture, and continue to heat until all the ingredients have melted and are thoroughly mixed together.

3 Add the dissolved gelatine mixture to the icing sugar, along with the egg white. Fit the beater to the machine and turn it on at its lowest speed. Beat until mixed, then increase the speed to maximum and continue beating until the paste is white and stringy.

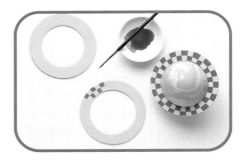

Tip

Slightly dampen your fingers when making flowers with petal (or flower) paste. This will prevent them drying before you have finished making them.

4 Remove the paste from the bowl and rub a thin layer of white fat over it to prevent the surface drying out. Place in a polythene bag and store in an airtight container. Allow the paste to rest and mature for at least 12 hours before using it.

SUGAR GLUE

To stick sugar pieces together, a sugar glue is required. Water can be used, but it is usually not quite strong enough to stick the pieces securely. Egg white makes a very good glue, as does royal icing; alternatively, a glue made from gum arabic is popular. Mix 1 teaspoon gum arabic powder with a few drops of water to make a thick paste. Store in an airtight container in the refrigerator.

To stick sugar pieces together successfully, only slightly dampen the paste surface with sugar glue, using a fine paintbrush. If you apply too much, your modelled piece may slide out of place. Gently press in position, holding for a few moments. If necessary, small pieces of foam sponge can be used to support glued pieces until they are dry and securely stuck.

MODELLING PASTE

Modelling paste is sugarpaste (rolled fondant) with a gum additive. When the gum is incorporated, it makes the paste firm but pliable so it is easier to work with. Items modelled from modelling paste will dry harder and also keep their shape.

A natural gum called gum tragacanth, which is widely used in the food industry, is usually used to make modelling paste. A man-made alternative called carboxy methyl cellulose (CMC) is cheaper than gum tragacanth and also goes further.

However, if you do not want to make your own modelling paste before embarking on the projects in this book, there are some ready-made modelling pastes available that give good results. Even more useful, they can be obtained pre-coloured.

All items are available from cake decorating suppliers.

Makes about 500g (1lb)
2 teaspoons gum tragacanth
500g (1lb) sugarpaste (rolled fondant)

1 Put the gum tragacanth on a work surface and knead it into the sugarpaste.

2 Double wrap the modelling paste in polythene or cling film (plastic wrap) and store in an airtight container for at least an hour before use.

Techniques

PAINTING ON SUGAR
Colour strengths

You can dilute food colouring pastes with cool boiled water. The amount of water added dictates the strength of the colour achieved. For a really pale, watercolour effect, dilute the colouring until very pale and transparent. For a stronger colour, only add a few drops of water until the food colouring paste is liquid enough to paint with.

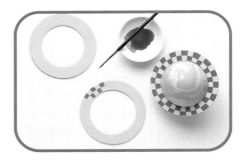

Applying colour

When painting on sugar, the brush must be kept only slightly damp to avoid paint running or even the sugar melting. Blot excess liquid from the paintbrush using a dry cloth or some absorbent kitchen paper. If you are nervous about painting, practise on a sheet of plain paper first. Remember, any painted mistakes on sugar can be removed with a damp cloth.

If a strong, solid colour is required, apply two to three thin coats, letting each coat dry thoroughly before applying the next. Keep brushstrokes to a minimum so the coat underneath doesn't begin to lift.

Mixing colours

To make a different shade of one colour, you can add a minute amount of another colour, e.g. if you have a basic green and want a bright grass green, add a touch of yellow. Likewise, if you are using basic green and you want a dark, muddy leaf green, add a touch of brown. Experimenting is part of the fun of painting on sugar, but if you are nervous about mixing your own colours, use different shades of the same colour from the vast range of food colouring pastes available.

Watch your modelled figures come to life at the end of each stage of painting.

Stippling

Stippling food colouring on to paste is a simple, effective and controllable method of adding colour. Preferably use a medium-sized, firm bristle paintbrush and only collect a little diluted food colouring on to the tip. Blot excess liquid off the brush with a cloth or absorbent kitchen paper, then repeatedly dot over the surface of the paste, keeping the paintbrush vertical.

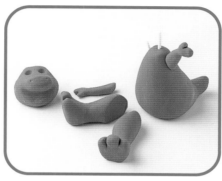

gently push on the head, using sugar glue to secure. An alternative to sugar stick supports are lengths of raw dried spaghetti. Never use cocktail sticks (toothpicks) as supports; they are sharp and could cause injury.

SHAPING CAKES

Balance

When building up a high cake, make sure each layer is completely straight and that the cake is perfectly balanced. If part of the cake is left only slightly uneven it will look much worse when covered with sugarpaste, and may cause the cake to lean.

MAKING HANDS

Model a teardrop of paste, then flatten slightly. Make a cut for a thumb on one side and pull it down a little, out of the way. Next, make three straight cuts along the top for the fingers, not quite as deep as the thumb. Twist each finger to lengthen and round off the end. Put the modelled hand in your palm, palm side up, then press gently on the centre, pulling downwards towards the wrist. This will give the hand a natural curve.

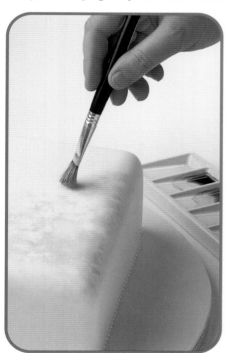

SUGAR STICKS

Sugar supports for models can be made from leftover modelling paste, or preferably pastillage (see page 9). Roll thin sticks or cut strips of paste in different lengths (roughly 5–7.5cm/2–3 inches) and leave to dry thoroughly before use. To support your modelled figures, insert a sugar stick down into the body, then

Cake sculpting

To sculpt cake into different shapes, use a sharp, serrated knife. Cut a little at a time, shaving off small pieces until you have the required shape. If you shave off more than you need, pieces can be stuck back on with a little buttercream, but take care not to do this too much as it may cause the sugarpaste to slip when applied.

Tip

For natural-looking fingernails, press the end of a piece of raw dried spaghetti into the tip of each finger to indent.

Cake Quantities Chart

Cake designs	Wallace & Gromit (page 64) Rugrats (page 72)	Garfield (page 40)	The Wombles (page 24) Babar (page 80)	Barney (page 88)
Bakeware	25cm (10in) square tin (pan)	two 1 litre (2pt/5 cup) ovenproof bowls	25cm (10in) square tin (pan)	25x20cm (10x8in) oblong tin (pan)
Self-raising flour	440g (14oz/3 ½ cups)	375g (12oz/3 cups)	375g (12oz/3 cups)	375g (12oz/3 cups)
Plain (all-purpose) flour	220g (7oz/1¾ cups)	185g (6oz/1 ½ cups)	185g (6oz/1 ½ cups)	185g (6oz/1 ½ cups)
Butter or soft margarine	440g (14oz/1¾ cups)	375g (12oz/1 ½ cups)	375g (12oz/1 ½ cups)	375g (12oz/1 ½ cups)
Caster (superfine) sugar	440g (14oz/1¾ cups)	375g (12oz/1 ½ cups)	375g (12oz/1 ½ cups)	375g (12oz/1 ½ cups)
Eggs (large)	7	6	6	6
Baking time	1–1¼ hours	1¼–1½ hours	1 hour	1–1¼ hours

Cake designs	Sesame Street (page 84)	My Little Pony (page 28)	Brambly Hedge (page 51)	Sonic the Hedgehog (page 47)
Bakeware	30x20cm (12x8in) oblong tin (pan)	20cm (8in) & 23cm (9in) round tins (pans)	20cm (8in) & 15cm (6in) round tins (pans)	3 litre (6pt/13 cup) ovenproof bowl
Self-raising flour	440g (14oz/3½ cups)	500g (1lb/4 cups)	440g (14oz/3 ½ cups)	375g (12oz/3 cups)
Plain (all-purpose) flour	220g (7oz/1¾ cups)	250g (8oz/2 cups)	220g (7oz/1 ¾ cups)	185g (6oz/1½ cups)
Butter or soft margarine	440g (14oz/1¾ cups)	500g (1lb/2 cups)	440g (14oz/1¾ cups)	375g (12oz/1½ cups)
Caster (superfine) sugar	440g (14oz/1¾ cups)	500g (1lb/2 cups)	440g (14oz/1¾ cups)	375g (12oz/1½ cups)
Eggs (large)	7	8	7	6
Baking time	1–1¼ hours	50 mins	1 ¼ hours (large) 1 hour (small)	1½ hours

Rupert (page 77)	Kipper (page 36)	The Flower Fairies (page 19)	Super Mario (page 60)
two 1 litre (2pt/5 cup) ovenproof bowls	23cm (9in) round tin (pan) & two 220ml (7fl oz) ovenproof bowls (¾ fill each bowl; remaining mixture in tin)	20cm (8in) square tin (pan)	1 litre (2pt/5 cup) & 750ml (1¼ pt/3 cup) ovenproof bowls (¾ fill each bowl)
315g (10oz/2½ cups)	500g (1lb/4 cups)	315g (10oz/2½ cups)	315g (10oz/2½ cups)
155g (5oz/1¼ cups)	250g (8oz/2 cups)	155g (5oz/1¼ cups)	155g (5oz/1¼ cups)
315g (10oz/1¼ cups)	500g (1lb/2 cups)	315g (10oz/1¼ cups)	315g (10oz/1¼ cups)
315g (10oz/1¼ cups)	500g (1lb/2 cups)	315g (10oz/1¼ cups)	315g (10oz/1¼ cups)
5	8	5	5
1¼ hours	30 mins (bowls) 1¼ hours (tin)	1 hour	1½ hours (large) 1 hour (small)

Fireman Sam (page 14)	Bananas in Pyjamas (page 56)	Little Miss (page 43) Gromit (page 69)	Dennis & Gnasher (page 32)
23cm (9in) square tin (pan)	30cm (12in) square tin (pan)	30cm (12in) square tin (pan)	2 litre (4pt/10 cup) ovenproof bowl
375g (12oz/3 cups)	500g (1lb/4 cups)	440g (14oz/3½ cups)	315g (10oz/2½ cups)
185g (6oz/1½ cups)	250g (8oz/2cups)	220g (7oz/1¾ cups)	155g (5oz/1¼ cups)
375g (12oz/1½ cups)	500g (1lb/2 cups)	440g (14oz/1¾ cups)	315g (10oz/1¼ cups)
375g (12oz/1½ cups)	500g (1lb/2 cups)	440g (14oz/1¾ cups)	315g (10oz/1¼ cups)
6	8	7	5
1¼ hours	1 hour	50 mins	1½ hours

FiREMAN SAM™

Children's hero Fireman Sam always likes to keep his fire engine, Jupiter, bright and clean.

MATERIALS

23cm (9 inch) square cake (see page 13)
30cm (12 inch) hexagonal cake board
75g (2½oz) pastillage
1.2kg (2lb 6½oz) sugarpaste (rolled fondant)
375g (12oz) buttercream
440g (14oz) modelling paste
30g (1oz) very soft royal icing
black, dark blue, red, flesh, brown, yellow and white food colouring pastes
cool boiled water
sugar glue

EQUIPMENT

large and small rolling pins
sharp knife
ruler
5mm (¼ inch) and 2.5cm (1 inch) square cutters
1cm (½ inch), 2.5cm (1 inch) and 4cm (1½ inch) circle cutters
cocktail sticks (toothpicks)
fine paintbrush
cake smoother
card for templates
bone tool
pieces of foam
paper piping bag

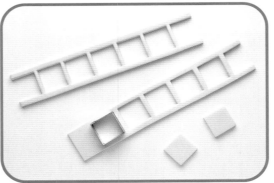

LADDER & BOARD

1 Colour the pastillage pale blue-grey using a touch each of the black and dark blue food colouring pastes. To make a ladder, first roll out and cut a strip measuring 20x4cm (8x1½ inches). Using a 2.5cm (1 inch) square cutter, cut out the ladder treads. Make another ladder, then put both aside to dry on a completely flat surface. Colour 625g (1¼lb) sugarpaste pale blue-grey as before. Roll out 440g (14oz) and cover the cake board, trimming excess from the edges. Put aside to dry.

JUPITER

2 Trim the crust from the cake and slice the top flat. Cut the cake exactly in half and put one half on top of the other. To heighten the cab of the engine, make a cut halfway along in the top of the cake 1cm (½ inch) deep. From this cut, slice out a wedge of cake, slicing towards the back of the engine. Position this wedge of cake on top of the cab.

Trim the top of the cake to round off the back of the cab. To shape the windscreen and front of the cab, cut down from the top at an outward angle to the top of the bottom layer. Using buttercream, sandwich the layers together, then spread a thin layer of buttercream over the surface of the cake to help the sugarpaste stick. Position the cake on the cake board.

3 Colour 75g (2½oz) sugarpaste black. Roll out and cut a strip measuring 2.5x60cm (1x24 inches). Carefully roll up, position against the bottom of the cake, then unravel around the base. Thinly roll out the trimmings and cut two circles using a 4cm (1½ inch) circle cutter. Cut each circle in half and position the four half circles above the black strip for the background of each wheel. Roll out 125g (4oz) of the blue-grey sugarpaste and cut out an oblong measuring 18x10cm (7x4 inches). Position against the back of the engine, leaving a gap of at least 1cm (½ inch) above the cake board, then smooth up the back and over the top to cover up to the engine cab. Mark lines on the back of the engine (see back-view photograph on

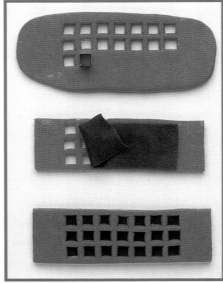

page 18) using the back of a knife, and use the knife handle to indent the top right-hand corner. Colour 500g (1lb) sugarpaste red. Roll out 155g (5oz) and cut out an oblong measuring 18x10cm (7x4 inches). Position against the front of the engine, leaving a gap at the base as before, and smooth up the front and over the top of the cab. To cover a side of the engine, moisten the edge of the red covering on the cab with sugar glue, then roll out 170g (5½oz) red sugarpaste and cut an oblong measuring 21x9cm (8½x3½ inches). Trim the top part of the left-hand side to taper slightly, then carefully lift and position against the right-hand side of the engine. Smooth the sugarpaste up to meet the top part of the cab and rub gently to remove the join. To neaten the edges of the side, smooth with a cake smoother. Make the opposite side in the same way, trimming the top part of the right-hand side to taper in slightly instead. Trim out the four wheel arches to uncover the black underneath, then mark lines for the doors on the cab and around the wheels using the back of a knife. Make indentations with your finger for the door handles on either side.

THE CAB

4 For the bonnet, windscreen and side windows, trace the outlines on page 91 and make card templates. Position the templates against the engine and cut around, removing the red sugarpaste. Roll out the remaining blue-grey sugarpaste and cut out the windscreen and two side windows using the templates. Slot into place, sticking with a little sugar glue. Colour 30g (1oz) modelling paste black. Using 15g (½oz), thinly roll out and cut strips to edge the windscreen and

side windows, sticking with sugar glue. Colour 75g (2½oz) modelling paste red. To make the grille, roll out 22g (¾oz) red modelling paste and cut an oblong measuring 11x2.5cm (4½x1 inch). Using a 5mm (¼ inch) square cutter, cut out squares, leaving a 2cm (¾ inch) gap at either end. Using 7g (¼oz) black modelling paste, thinly roll out and cut a piece to cover the reverse side of the grille, sticking in place with sugar glue. Stick the grille on the front of the engine, leaving a gap for the bumper. Using the card template, make the bonnet from 22g (¾oz) red modelling paste and stick in place, resting on top of the grille.

WHEELS, DOORS & LIGHTS

5 To make the wheels, colour 125g (4oz) modelling paste dark grey using black food colouring paste. Divide into

four pieces. Roll each into a ball, flatten slightly, then indent the centres using the 2.5cm (1 inch) circle cutter. To make the hubs, thinly roll out 7g (¼oz) each of white and red modelling paste. Cut two circles of each colour, cut into quarters, then stick alternate colours on the centre of each wheel. Roll four small red balls for the wheel centres and stick in place. Using sugar glue, stick each wheel in place. Colour 60g (2oz) modelling paste pale grey. Thinly roll out and cut the six storage doors for the engine sides (see photo on page 18). Mark the lines with the back of a knife. Lift carefully and stick in position with a little sugar glue. Using the remaining grey modelling paste, make the bases for the two front and back siren lights, the headlights, the bumper with bumper bars, the base of the two indicator lights, two wing mirrors, two door handles and two foot rails, sticking everything in position with sugar glue, then model ten tiny buttons for Fireman Sam's tunic, indenting the centre of each with a cocktail stick, and cut a tiny square of grey for his belt buckle.

FIREMAN SAM

6 Colour 45g (1½oz) modelling paste dark blue, 40g (1¼oz) yellow, 7g (¼oz) flesh and 7g (¼oz) brown. You can either build Fireman Sam up piece by piece in his pose against Jupiter, or make him flat (as in the step photograph on page 17) and position him when dry. First model two teardrop shapes for his shoes using 7g (¼oz) black modelling paste split in half. Using 22g (¾oz) yellow modelling paste, model a fat sausage shape, then cut it along three-quarters of its length to separate the legs. Flatten the ends of the trousers and down the sides to remove the ridges, and pinch each leg

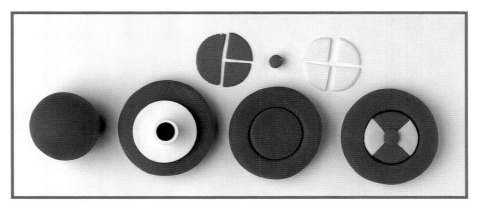

With the remaining flesh-coloured paste, make two tiny ears, a bulbous nose and two hands (see page 11). Using 7g (¼oz) yellow paste, make Fireman Sam's helmet by first rolling a ball, then hollowing out the underside by pushing in with your finger. Pinch around the edge to pull out the rim, then pinch along the top for the ridge. Make flattened teardrop shapes using the brown modelling paste for Fireman Sam's hair. Stick in place over his head and stick two pieces on the underside of his helmet so that they flick up over the rim. Make Sam's eyes using white, brown and black modelling paste; model tiny flattened balls and stick in place using a little sugar glue. With a little more black modelling paste, thinly roll out and cut a strip for his belt and a tiny square for the centre of the buckle. Stick in place with the buckle made earlier. Stick Sam's buttons in place.

7 With the remaining red modelling paste, thinly roll out and cut strips for the back of the engine, sticking in place with sugar glue. Model two flattened balls for the top of the engine, and make the

halfway down for the knees. Stick on to the shoes using sugar glue. Model 22g (¾oz) dark blue paste into Sam's body, hollowing out the base by pinching around the edge, enough to sit over the trousers. Model the two sleeves from 7g (¼oz) dark blue, using a bone tool to hollow out the end of each so the hands will slot in. Model a flattened ball for the neck and thinly roll out and cut two shoulder strips. Stick in place with sugar glue. If necessary, use foam pieces to support Fireman Sam whilst drying. To make Fireman Sam's head, roll a teardrop shape with flesh-coloured modelling paste and stick on to the neck with the narrow end upwards.

bucket, hollowing out slightly at the top. Thinly roll out red and yellow paste and cut strips for the warning signs on the back of the engine. Stick alternate coloured strips together, then cut two squares and stick in place. With a little grey modelling paste make the bucket handle. With the remaining yellow modelling paste, make a bell for the top of the engine and model two sponges, marking each with a cocktail stick. Using white modelling paste, model a flattened ball for Fireman Sam's helmet badge, roll out and cut the licence plate and then make the white and orange indicator light at the front by mixing a little red and yellow paste together. With the remaining dark blue, make the siren lights for the top, front and back of the engine. Thinly roll out and cut two 1cm (½ inch) circles and stick on to the doors on either side of the engine. With the white colouring paste and a fine paint-brush, paint the shield on either side.

8 Dilute a tiny amount of black food colouring paste with water. Paint a streaky effect over the windscreen and side windows. Add a little more colour, then paint the steering wheel and J999 on the licence plate. Paint in Fireman Sam's smile. Dilute a tiny amount of red food colouring paste with water, then paint the star design on Fireman

Sam's helmet. Colour half the royal icing palest blue. Stir into the remaining royal icing until streaky. Pour into a piping bag and snip a hole in the tip. Pipe the 'water' into the bucket, over the cake board and sponge, then pipe all the drips. When the ladders are completely dry, stick on top of the engine using a little soft royal icing to secure.

THE FLOWER FAIRIES™

Inspired by Cicely Mary Barker's exquisite watercolour illustrations and poems published from 1923, the enchanted world of the Flower Fairies is represented in a delicately decorated cake.

MATERIALS

20cm (8 inch) square cake (see page 13)
36cm (14 inch) round cake board
1.25kg (2½ lb) sugarpaste (rolled fondant)
410g (13oz) buttercream
60g (2oz) royal icing
100g (3½oz) petal paste
125g (4oz) modelling paste
blue, mauve, brown, flesh, pink, yellow, brown, green, red and black food colouring pastes
cool boiled water
sugar glue
sugar sticks (see page 11) or raw dried spaghetti

EQUIPMENT

large and small rolling pins
cake smoother
greaseproof paper piping bags
no. 1 plain piping tube (tip)
large firm bristle paintbrush
pieces of foam
fine and medium paintbrushes
small and large leaf veiners or dried bay leaves
miniature calyx cutter
medium and large rose leaf cutters
sharp pointed scissors
cocktail sticks (toothpicks)

CAKE & BOARD

1 Roll out 500g (1lb) sugarpaste and use to cover the cake board. Put aside to dry. Trim the crust from the cake and split and fill with buttercream. Spread a thin layer of buttercream over the surface of the cake to help the sugarpaste stick. Position the cake on the cake board. Roll out the remaining sugarpaste and cover the cake. Polish with a cake smoother. Using one-third of the royal icing and a no. 1 piping tube, pipe a snail's trail around the base of the cake, then leave the cake to dry. Dilute a little blue and mauve food colouring separately using cool boiled water. Spread out the bristles of the firm paintbrush by pressing down on to a hard surface. Moisten the tip of the brush with diluted food colouring, dab any excess off on absorbent kitchen paper, then stipple the colours, one at a time, over the surface of the board and cake.

WHITE BINDWEED

2 Make the flowers using 15g (½oz) petal paste. Model a teardrop shape, then push the end of a paintbrush down into the centre of the large end. Using your fingers, pinch around the edge to open up the flower, making the edge quite thin. Press the side of a paintbrush around the inside to indent, then smooth the top edge to curve around. Make the second flower in the same way. Use 7g (¼oz) petal paste to make the stamens, calyxes and stems. Each flower centre has five stamens which are thin sausages of paste about 1cm (½ inch) long. Make the last stamen a little longer with a rounded end, and split the end by making a cut in the centre. Bunch the stamens together with the longer one in the centre, and stick in position using a little royal icing. Using the bindweed calyx template (see page 92), roll out some petal paste and cut out three shapes for each calyx. Stick around the base of

each flower. Model two thin stems by rolling sausages of petal paste that are slightly fuller at one end. Stick the stems in position with sugar glue, placing the fuller end against the base of each flower.

BINDWEED FAIRY

3 First make the dress (body) using 7g (¼oz) modelling paste. Make a teardrop shape, hollowing out the base for the legs and keeping the bottom area rounded. Press into the back to indent a curve, and press into the top with your finger to curve the neck and chest. Mark pleats with a cocktail stick. Using another 7g (¼oz), first make two tiny sleeves, hollowing out the ends with the end of a paintbrush so the arms can slot in, and make the knees by modelling two teardrop shapes to stick to the underside of the front of the dress.

Stick the fairy on the top of the cake. Model two small oval shapes for the feet and stick in place with one slightly more underneath the dress than the other. Make the arms by rolling sausage shapes 2.5cm (1 inch) long, pinching each at one end to indent the wrists, which will then round off the hands. Press each hand a little flat and cut the fingers (see page 11). Halfway along the arm, press in the centre and pinch out behind to make the elbow. Cut off the top of each arm and twist to a point. Using sugar glue, stick the flowers in place with one resting on the fairy's dress, then stick each arm in place, resting on the flower.

Model a thin neck and push a 2.5cm (1 inch) sugar stick or piece of spaghetti through the centre so the stick protrudes evenly at each end. Using sugar glue, stick the neck into the top of the dress. Make the fairy's head and nose by first rolling a ball, then pinching the base to point the chin. Roll the side of a paintbrush at the eye area to indent and shape the face. Using sugar glue to secure, lower the head down on to the sugar stick. Make a minute nose and stick in place using sugar glue, smoothing the join. Using the hat leaf and wing templates (see page 92), thinly roll out 7g (¼oz) petal paste and cut out two leaves for the hat, pressing into the small leaf veiner to shape. Cut out two wings. Stick the leaves on to the fairy's head with a tiny modelled stalk on top, then stick her wings in place and support with pieces of foam while drying.

To make the bindweed leaves, thinly roll out 7g (¼oz) petal paste and cut four leaf shapes using the template (see page 92). Press each leaf on to the centre of the large leaf veiner to indent, then curl slightly. With the trimmings, roll long thin sausages of paste to make stalks and binders, twisting them around each other, with some binders curling upwards. Assemble on top of the cake and use pieces of foam for support while drying.

BLACK MEDICK GIRL FAIRY

4 Use 7g (¼oz) modelling paste to make a dress as for the Bindweed Fairy, but curve the front of this dress around to look like the fairy's knees are covered. To make her puffed sleeves, model two small balls of modelling paste and mark pleats with a cocktail stick. Model two tiny flattened balls for her cuffs and assemble on to the dress. Push the end of a paintbrush into each cuff to indent so the arms will slot in. Thinly roll out 7g (¼oz) petal paste and, using the templates on page 92, cut out four girl fairy wings and two leaves for the front and back of her dress. Indent the leaves with the small veiner to shape, then stick in place with the fairy wings and use foam pieces for support while drying. Thinly roll out the trimmings and cut out a miniature calyx for the fairy's collar, and stick on top of her dress. Using 7g (¼oz) modelling paste, make the fairy's shoes (feet), arms and hands, neck, head and nose as made for the Bindweed Fairy, securing with sugar glue. Colour 15g (½oz) royal icing brown. Put half into a piping bag, cut a small hole in the tip and pipe the fairy's hair.

BLACK MEDICK BOY FAIRY

5 First make his trousers and top using 7g (¼oz) modelling paste. For his trousers (see overleaf), model a sausage and flatten slightly. Make a cut along three-quarters of its length to separate the legs. Smooth out and bend into a kneeling position, with the top of the trousers facing forwards not upwards. To make his top, model a teardrop shape and flatten slightly. Make small cuts either side for the sleeves. Smooth out ridges, then stick on top of the trousers. Using 7g (¼oz) modelling paste, make the shoes, arms and hands, neck, head and nose as before, again supporting with foam pieces while drying. Using 7g (¼oz) petal paste and the boy wing templates (see page 92), thinly roll out and cut four wings, sticking in place as before, then thinly roll out and cut out a headscarf using the template on page 92. Stick the widest edge around the fairy's face, twisting the back into a point.

Use 7g (¼oz) petal paste to make black medick stalks and leaves. Roll thin sausages for the stalks and stick against the side of the cake with tiny modelled leaves at the joins. Stick the fairies in place, then thinly roll out some petal paste and cut out larger leaves using the template on page 92. Mark the vein of each leaf using the small veiner. Using 15g (½oz)

royal icing and the no. 1 piping tube, pipe all the little round and oval-shaped flowers and seeds in bunches. Pipe a line around the girl fairy's head and pipe small bunches of flowers for her crown. Pipe a small bunch of flowers for the boy fairy's hat bobble.

MULBERRY FAIRY

6 To make the leaves, twigs and berries, first model a 7g (¼oz) flattened ball of modelling paste to support the leaf the fairy is sitting on, and stick on to the cake board against the side of the cake. Using 15g (½oz) petal paste and the rose leaf cutters, cut out two leaves. Trim the top of each leaf using the mulberry leaf templates on page 92, then indent veins with the large leaf veiner. Stick the larger leaf over the flattened ball and the top of the smaller leaf against the side of the cake. Model a long twig with a knot, a small twig that the fairy is sitting on, and all the berries. Put the small twig aside for later and stick everything else in place as soon as it is made. To make the knot for the long twig, stick on a minute ball of paste and

push the tip of a cocktail stick into it to make a hole. For the berries, stick a pea-sized ball of paste in place and stick tiny balls over the surface, pressing each slightly flat.

To make the Mulberry Fairy, use 7g (¼oz) modelling paste to make his trousers and top. Make his trousers as for the Black Medick Boy Fairy, keeping the legs straight. Model a teardrop-shaped body and sausage-shaped sleeves (the waistcoat is made later). Indent the end of each sleeve by pushing in the end of a paintbrush so the hands will slot in. Sugar glue in position as each piece is made. Stick the small twig under the fairy. Using 7g (¼oz) modelling paste, make the hands (see page 11), shoes

with little bobbles and thinly roll out and cut two calyxes for his collar. Make his head and nose as for the other fairies. Model two pointed ears, indenting the centre of each with the end of a paint-brush, and model a dome-shaped hat with a little stalk on top. Pipe his curly hair using the remaining brown royal icing. Using the waistcoat and wing templates on page 92, thinly roll out 7g (¼oz) petal paste and cut out the waistcoat and four wings. Stick in place with sugar glue.

HORSE CHESTNUT FAIRY

7 Make the branches and three chestnuts first. Using 7g (¼oz) modelling paste, roll a long uneven sausage and cut two smaller branches from the length. Stick the long branch against the side of the cake with the two smaller ones, marking lines with a knife. Make a knot in the twig as for the Mulberry Fairy. Divide 15g (½oz) modelling paste into three pieces. Roll one into a ball and snip up prickles with scissors. Stick on the end of the second twig. For the split chestnuts, divide a second piece of paste in two and roll two balls for the conkers. Split the remaining piece into four and model four dome shapes for the chestnut skins, snipping prickles as before. Stick over the conkers, letting some of each

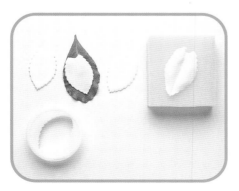

22

conker show, and stick in place on the ends of the remaining twigs.

To make the Horse Chestnut Fairy, first model two sausages of paste for his legs using 7g (¼oz) modelling paste. Roll the ends of each a little narrower for the ankles and pinch in halfway along to indent the backs of the knees, pinching out at the front to shape the knees. Stick the back leg in place along the twig, then bend the remaining leg, rounding off the top for the fairy's bottom. Stick this leg in place, securing the ankle against the side of the twig. Using 7g (¼oz) modelling paste, shape a piece for the fairy's top and make the sleeves, cuffs, hands, shoes, head and nose as for the other fairies. Model the chestnut hat and snip prickles as before, sticking in place with sugar glue. Using 7g (¼oz) petal paste and the template for the Horse Chestnut Fairy wings (see page 92), thinly roll out and cut two wings. Stick in position against the side of the cake.

CANDYTUFT FAIRY

8 Use 7g (¼oz) petal paste to make all the flowers, leaves and stalks. For the leaves, thinly roll out some petal paste and cut out two leaves using the template on page 92. Carefully fold each leaf in half to mark the vein. Model a stalk and stick in position using sugar glue. To make a flower, model a teardrop shape and press the end of a paintbrush into the large end. Make four even cuts around the edge, then remove the paintbrush. Pinch each petal until thin and slightly curled. You might need to push the end of the paintbrush into the centre again to reshape, then trim off any excess paste at the base. Make 30 flowers in various sizes and stick in groups on the cake board and stalk.

Make the Candytuft Fairy's shorts and top using 7g (¼oz) modelling paste. For her shorts, model a ball and flatten slightly. Make a small cut to separate the legs of the shorts, then hollow out for the fairy's legs to slot in. Bend into a sitting position and stick in place against the side of the cake. Make the teardrop-shaped top as before but without any sleeves. With the remaining modelling paste, make the fairy's legs. Roll a sausage and pinch to shape the ankle, making the end rounded. Pinch to shape a foot. Mark tiny toes. Halfway along the length of the leg, pinch in the back to bend and pinch out at the front to shape the knee. Make another leg and stick both in position. Model the fairy's arms and hands, neck, head and nose as before. With the remaining petal paste and the Candytuft Fairy wings templates (see page 92), thinly roll out and cut four wings. With the trimmings, model four tiny petals and stick in position with the fairy wings. Put the remaining royal icing in a piping bag, cut a small hole in the tip, and pipe the hair for the Candytuft, Bindweed and the Black Medick Boy Fairies.

PAINTING

9 The cake is ready for painting after a few hours. Refer to pages 10–11 before you begin. Use the fine and medium-sized paintbrushes and as the Flower Fairies are watercolour paintings, keep your colours quite pale and watery. To highlight the fairies, a little colour is stippled behind or beneath them using the medium paintbrush. Remember, you have 'drawn' your 'picture' by modelling the figures; all you have to do now is colour it in.

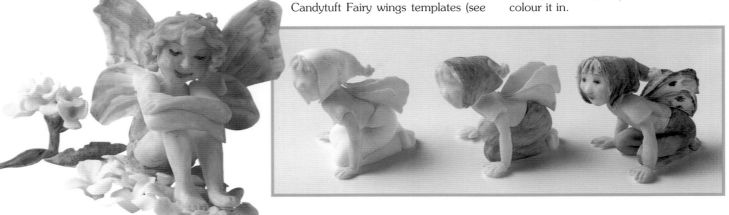

The WOMBLES™

Still 'Wombling Free' on the common, The Wombles of Wimbledon continue to be as popular as ever!

MATERIALS

25cm (10 inch) square cake (see page 12)
30cm (12 inch) round cake board
1.25kg (2½lb) sugarpaste (rolled fondant)
45g (1½oz) pastillage
625g (1¼lb) modelling paste
440g (14oz) buttercream
125g (4oz) royal icing
green, mauve, yellow, golden brown, red, black, blue and dark brown food colouring pastes
sugar glue
dark green dusting powder (petal dust/blossom tint)
pale green pollen dust
cool boiled water

EQUIPMENT

large rolling pin
small piece of voile net
sharp knife
piping bags
small circle cutter
bone tool
fine and medium paintbrushes
2.5cm (1 inch) circle cutter
scissors
pieces of foam

Tip

To give The Wombles' heads extra support, insert sugar sticks (see page 11) when sticking the heads in place.

BOARD & PASTILLAGE PIECES

1 Colour 375g (12oz) sugarpaste green. Roll out and cover the cake board, trimming excess from the edge. To give a subtle grass effect, texture the surface by pressing a piece of voile net over the surface with a rolling pin. Using pastillage, roll out and cut a strip for the awning over the door measuring 9x3cm (3½ x1¼ inches), and roll two thin posts measuring 10cm (4 inches) in length. Make the flag and pole in one piece. Roll 15 small, thin, uneven sausages of pastillage to make the twigs for the fire, marking along each one with a knife. Put everything aside to dry.

15cm (6 inches)	7.5cm (3 inches)
13cm (5 inches) base	roof
13cm (5 inches) middle	roof

CAKE

2 Trim the crust from the cake and slice the top flat. Cut the cake as shown in the diagram. Assemble the layers with the two small roof pieces sitting side by side on top of the two larger pieces. Trim the top layer to make a sloped roof. Using buttercream, sandwich the layers together, then spread a thin layer of buttercream over the cake to help the sugarpaste stick.

TENT

3 Colour 750g (1½lb) sugarpaste mauve. Roll out and cover the cake completely, pulling up a pleat at the

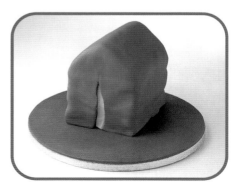

front. Cut excess away, leaving a gap to make the opening for the door. Reserve the mauve trimmings. Press in around the tent using your hands to mark an uneven fabric effect. Position the cake on the cake board. Colour 22g (¾oz) modelling paste yellow. Using 7g (¼oz), fill the opening at the door.

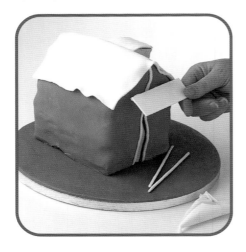

4 Moisten the roof with a little sugar glue. Thinly roll out the remaining white sugarpaste and cut an 18cm (7 inch) square. Lift and cover the roof completely, pinching around the edge to thin and frill. Make a small hole in the front. Using the trimmings, thinly roll strips and stick in place around the door opening. With the mauve sugarpaste trimmings, model a wedge for the roof window, sticking with sugar glue. Using 30g (1oz) white modelling paste, thinly roll out and cut pieces to cover the sides and top of the roof window. Using a little royal icing to secure, stick the pastillage awning in place with the posts supporting it.

Cut two strips of white modelling paste, one for the overhanging edge above the roof window and the other for the overhanging edge of the awning. Using the small circle cutter, cut out the scalloped pattern along one edge of each strip. Stick in place using sugar glue. With the trimmings, cut a tiny square for the patch on the awning, and put aside. Colour 15g (½oz) modelling paste mauve. Thinly roll out and cut thick and thin strips to decorate the awning and roof window, sticking in place with sugar glue. Stick the patch in place. Dust the surface of the cake board with dark green dusting powder and sprinkle with pale green pollen dust.

ORINOCO

5 Colour 250g (8oz) modelling paste golden brown, 140g (4½oz) red, 22g (¾oz) black and 100g (3½oz) blue. Model a small pillow using 22g (¾oz) white modelling paste. Using 60g (2oz) golden brown modelling paste, roll a ball for Orinoco's body and make his two legs, one arm and a hand (see page 11). Using 30g (1oz) golden brown paste, shape Orinoco's teardrop-shaped head, making the muzzle quite pointed. Press in with the small end of a bone tool to indent the eyes. To make the ears, take a small piece of golden brown and model two flattened teardrop shapes, indenting in the centre of each with your finger. Fill the centres with flattened pieces of white modelling paste, then stick in place.

Using 15g (½oz) red modelling paste, make Orinoco's hat. Model a flattened circle and stick on top of his head. Shape the top of the hat, tapering it in at the base, and stick in place. To make Orinoco's eyes, roll two balls of white modelling paste and stick in place in the sockets. Using a minute amount of blue modelling paste, model irises for the eyes. Using black modelling paste, thinly roll out and cut a strip for the hat band, model a ball for his nose and two tiny pupils for his eyes. Model tiny eyelids using golden brown modelling paste. Thinly roll out 7g (¼oz) red modelling

paste and cut a strip for Orinoco's scarf. Make small cuts at either end to frill, then carefully wrap the scarf around his neck. Using white royal icing in a piping bag with a small hole cut in the tip, pipe the fur effect over Orinoco's body, flicking up the fur around his face.

WELLINGTON

6 To make Wellington peeking out at the tent door, model a teardrop-shaped head, the ears, nose and eyes as for Orinoco, but make the irises brown. Using a small piece of blue modelling paste, thinly roll out and cut a 2.5cm (1 inch) circle. Thinly roll out some black and cut another circle. Cut each circle in half, and cut two different-coloured halves into three pieces each. Stick alternate colours together to make the hat. Cut out a peak for the hat using black, and model a blue button for the top. Using 7g (¼oz) black modelling paste to make the neck fur, model a flattened circle and pinch around the edge. Stick everything in place using sugar glue, then stick Wellington in position using pieces of foam for support whilst drying. Pipe the fur using white royal icing.

BUNGO

7 To make Bungo at the roof window, make the head, ears, nose and eyes as before, but make the irises blue. Model a black hat, indenting with the side of a paintbrush, and cut a strip for the hat edging, sticking in place with sugar glue. Stick Bungo in place using foam pieces for support whilst drying.

Dilute a little black food colouring paste with water. Using a fine paintbrush, paint Wellington's glasses, the awning poles and checked design over the patch on the awning, and on the sides of the roof window. Dilute a little dark brown food colouring paste with

water, and paint the flag pole and all the twigs brown. Dilute a little red food colouring paste with water and paint the Wombles logo on to the flag using the template on page 91. Make a hole in the top of the cake by pushing in the end of a paintbrush, then slot in the flag pole.

ALDERNEY

8 Put aside a minute amount of blue modelling paste, then with the remaining piece model Alderney's sleeping-bag, pinching up the back for the rounded hood. Press a dip in the top for Alderney's head to sit in, then smooth the hood over. Make the neck fur, head, ears, hands, nose and eyes as before, but make the irises blue. Stick two balls of golden brown paste on either side of her head for her hair bunches. Colour 22g (¾oz) royal icing cream (using a touch of golden brown food colouring paste), then pipe her hair.

TOMSK

9 To make Tomsk, first make his sleeping-bag as before using 100g (3½oz) red modelling paste, but make the dip in the top deeper. Using 15g (½oz) golden brown modelling paste, model a

ball and fill the dip in the sleeping-bag for Tomsk's body. Thinly roll out a tiny amount of white modelling paste and cut out a 2.5cm (1 inch) square. Trim a curve in the top of the square to make Tomsk's vest and stick in place. Trim the vest with strips of red modelling paste. Using 7g (¼oz) golden brown modelling paste, model one arm and a hand and stick in place against the side of the sleeping-bag. Make the neck fur, head, ears, nose and eyes as before, making the irises brown. Colour 15g (½oz) royal icing grey and pipe the hair on Tomsk and Bungo. Using the remaining white royal icing, pipe the body fur.

FIRE

10 Colour 15g (½oz) modelling paste dark grey and model small flattened stones for around the fire. Add red food colouring paste to the remaining yellow modelling paste and knead until streaky. Using scissors, make cuts for the flames, pinching each to a point. Stick the stones around the base and the pastillage twigs against the flames using sugar glue.

My Little Pony®

As far away as you can imagine and as near as you can wish is Ponyland, the magical place of My Little Pony.

MATERIALS

20cm (8 inch) and 23cm (9 inch)
round cakes (see page 12)
30cm (12 inch) round cake board
1.6kg (3lb 3oz) sugarpaste (rolled
fondant)
440g (14oz) buttercream
500g (1lb) modelling paste
green, yellow, mauve, pink, golden
brown, blue, black and orange food
colouring pastes
cool boiled water
sugar glue

EQUIPMENT

large and small rolling pins
sharp knife
cake smoother
cocktail sticks (toothpicks)
medium heart cutter
5cm (2 inch) round cutter
2.5cm (1 inch) square cutter
large blossom plunger cutter
pieces of foam
small shell piping tube (tip)
fine paintbrush
black food colouring pen

Tip
After rolling out a large
piece of sugarpaste (rolled
fondant), lift it by folding it
over the rolling pin. This will
make it easier to position.

CAKES & BOARD

1 Colour 375g (12oz) sugarpaste grass green using green food colouring with a touch of yellow. Roll out and cover the cake board, trimming excess from the edge. Put aside to dry. Trim the crusts from both cakes, and slice the top flat on the smaller cake only. Trim the top of the larger cake, keeping the rounded shape where the cake has risen. Position the larger cake on top of the smaller one, then trim around the base of the larger cake to remove the ridge. Cut a slice about 2.5cm (1 inch) deep from the front of the cake to make a flatter area for the door and to make the roof higher at the front. Cut a layer in each cake and sandwich all layers together using buttercream, then spread a thin layer of buttercream over the surface of the cake to help the sugarpaste stick. Position the cake on the cake board. Cut and remove a wedge of sugarpaste from the board at the front of the cake, making it the width of the door, and widening at the cake board edge.

HOUSE

2 Roll out 875g (1¾lb) sugarpaste and cover the cake completely, smoothing around the shape with a smoother. Trim excess from around the base. Using the door template (see page 91) as a guide, cut and remove the door shape at the front of the cake 2cm (¾ inch) above the base. Colour 345g (11oz) sugarpaste yellow. To make the layered roof, thinly roll out 200g (6½oz) yellow paste and cover the top of the cake, trimming excess from around the edge. To frill the edge, make little downward cuts with a knife, slanting them slightly at the front. Using the remaining yellow sugarpaste, thinly roll out and cut the second layer for the roof. Position on top of the first layer and trim until slightly smaller, frilling the edge by making downward cuts directly on the roof. Thinly roll out the trimmings and cut a circle for the third layer, position on top of the cake and frill.

3 To make the door, first colour 60g (2oz) modelling paste yellow. Roll out half, marking lines on the surface with the back of a knife. Scratch finer wood-effect lines using a cocktail stick.

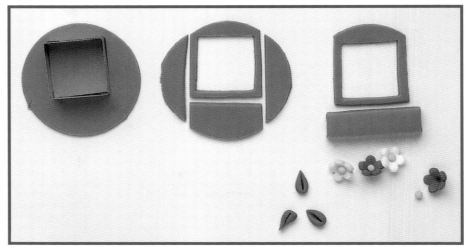

Position the door template (see page 91) on top and cut around. Lift the cut-out door and carefully slot it in position at the front of the cake. Press in the heart cutter and remove the piece of yellow modelling paste. Colour 60g (2oz) modelling paste pale grey and 7g (¼oz) grey. Roll out half the pale grey and cut a wedge to fit in the cut-out path section on the cake board. With the remaining pale grey, thickly roll out and cut two steps, making one double the width of the other. Stick the smaller step on top of the larger and stick in place against the cake with a little sugar glue. Model uneven flattened balls of paste for the path stones using the grey modelling paste, and stick over the surface of the path. Smooth with the cake smoother to inlay. Thinly roll out the yellow trimmings and cut out a door mat, sticking it on to the top step.

BUSHES, WINDOWS & FLOWERS

4 To make the bushes, colour 140g (4½oz) modelling paste green. Put aside 7g (¼oz), then pinch and shape the remainder to make different-sized bushes. Stick around the base of the cake and around the cake board edge. Colour 35g (1¼oz) modelling paste mauve. To make the window frames, thinly roll out 15g (½oz) and cut two circles with a 5cm (2 inch) cutter. From near the top of each circle cut out a square using a 2.5cm (1 inch) cutter. Keeping an arched top, trim around the sides and at the bottom to make the window frames. Thickly roll out 7g (¼oz) mauve modelling paste and cut two window-boxes, slightly wider than the window frames. Stick the windows and window-boxes in place.

To make the blossom flowers, first colour 22g (¾oz) modelling paste dark pink and 30g (1oz) pale pink. Using 7g (¼oz) each of the dark pink, pale pink, white, and the remaining yellow, roll out and cut all the blossom flowers using the blossom plunger cutter, shaping each flower by indenting with the end of a paintbrush on a piece of foam. Press the tip of the piping tube into the centre of each yellow flower to mark stamens. With the yellow trimmings, model little balls of paste for the centres of each of the remaining blossom flowers. Stick blossoms over the window-boxes and bushes, leaving some bushes uncovered for the roses later. With the remaining green modelling paste, make little teardrop-shaped leaves, indenting the centre of each with a cocktail stick, and roll a long thin sausage for the vine at the side of the door. Stick in place, curling over the top, with leaves along the length. Stick some more leaves on the window-boxes and roof.

WHITE PONY

5 Roll 45g (1½oz) white modelling paste into a sausage. Using the photograph below as a guide, pinch all the way around to shape the pony's head, twisting it up to create her neck. Keep the top part of her body small and her rump rounded. Shape a long, rounded muzzle and stick her head to her body. Mark her smile using the wide end of the piping tube, dimpling the corners with a cocktail stick. Indent two little holes either side of her nose with the tip of a cocktail stick. With 15g (½oz) white modelling paste, make her two front and back legs with little balls of paste stuck on the end of each for the hoofs, and two pointed ears. Press a minute ball of white paste flat, cut in half and stick either side of her head for her eyes. Using 7g (¼oz) mauve modelling paste, make her pupils by pressing minute balls of paste flat, then model sausages of paste for the bottom layer of her mane

30

and tail, tapering to points at each end and sticking in a curled position. Colour 15g (½oz) modelling paste golden brown. With 7g (¼oz) dark pink and all the golden brown modelling paste, make the middle and top layers of her mane and tail as before, modelling a curl of golden brown for her forelock.

BLUE & PURPLE PONIES

6 Colour 15g (½oz) modelling paste blue. Roll half of it into a ball, then shape a long, rounded muzzle. Make the ears and eyes, marking the smile and nose as for the white pony. Stick in position at the window, supported with a piece of foam until dry. Make her mane using the remaining mauve modelling paste and 15g (½oz) pale pink, sticking in place with sugar glue. Colour 7g (¼oz) modelling paste purple, using pink food colouring paste with a touch of blue, and colour 7g (¼oz) pink. Make the pony at the other window in the same way, using the purple modelling paste for her head and ears, all the pink and the remaining dark pink for her mane. Make the eyes as before but make them blue.

HOUSE DETAILS & ROSES

7 Thinly roll out 7g (¼oz) white modelling paste and cut out a heart, keeping it in the cutter. Position the cutter in the heart recess in the door and carefully push the cut-out heart into the recess. With the remaining white modelling

paste, roll a ball for the door light, creating a hole in the top with the end of a paintbrush for the light fitting to slot in. Using some of the remaining blue modelling paste, roll a tiny ball and a sausage for the light fitting. Bend the sausage at one end. Stick the tiny blue ball on to the cake and indent with the end of a paintbrush. Assemble the light using sugar glue to secure. Make the door lock and handle using the remaining blue modelling paste. Use the remaining pale pink modelling paste to make all the roses, using the photograph, above right, as a guide. Make 20 roses, sticking each in place as soon as it is made. Start by rolling a small sausage of paste and press it a little flat. Press and pull out along one edge to scallop and flatten petals. Turn over and moisten along the straight edge. Carefully roll up, keeping the rose petals level. Twist at the base to narrow and remove excess, then carefully turn the petals outwards using a damp paintbrush.

FINISHING

8 To finish, dilute a little black food colouring with some water. Using a fine paintbrush, paint the ponies' eyes, leaving a little unpainted star-shaped 'twinkle' in each. Paint the eyelashes and eyebrows. Draw the criss-cross pattern on the front door using the black food colouring pen. Separately dilute a minute amount of pink and golden brown food colouring paste with a little water and paint the heart design on the white pony's rump. Using the 'My Little Pony' logo (see page 28) as a template, transfer the outline on to the roof of the cake. Draw the lettering with the black food colouring pen, then using diluted food colouring, paint the rainbow.

31

DENNIS & GNASHER

MATERIALS

2 litre (4 pint/10 cup) bowl-shaped
cake (see page 13)
25cm (10 inch) round cake board
1.25kg (2½ lb) sugarpaste (rolled
fondant)
440g (14oz) buttercream
280g (9oz) modelling paste
green, yellow, golden brown, red and
black food colouring pastes
sugar glue

☆

EQUIPMENT

large and small rolling pins
sharp knife
large daisy cutter
no. 4 plain piping tube (tip)
paintbrush
bone tool

Tip

To prevent untidy edges
when cutting out the leaf
shapes with the daisy cutter,
rub the underside of the cutter with your fingertip to
remove any excess paste
before removing the shape
from the cutter.

**Always up to mischievous tricks with his dog
Gnasher, Dennis is as popular today as he was
when he first appeared in *The Beano*.**

BOARD & CAKE

1 Colour 315g (10oz) sugarpaste yellow-green using green food colouring paste with a touch of yellow. Roll out
and cover the cake board. Trim and put
aside to dry, reserving the trimmings.
Trim the crust from the cake, keeping
the top rounded where the cake has
risen. Slice two layers in the cake and
sandwich back together with buttercream. Turn the cake upside-down.
Spread a thin layer of buttercream over
the surface of the cake to help the
sugarpaste stick, and place on the centre
of the board.

2 Colour the remaining sugarpaste
green. Roll out 625g (1¼ lb) and
cover the cake, smoothing around the
shape and tucking the sugarpaste under.

3 Using the remaining green sugarpaste, roll out and cut daisy shapes
to make the leaves for the bush. Cut
each daisy shape in two to make groups
of five and three leaves. Stick over the

surface of the cake with sugar glue, starting at the base and working around in small clumps. Leave a space at the top for Dennis and Gnasher.

PEASHOOTER

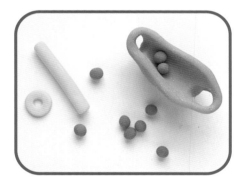

4 To make the peashooter, peas and bag, colour 7g (¼oz) modelling paste yellow and 7g (¼oz) golden brown. Using the yellow, model a flattened circle and cut out a small hole in the centre using the no. 4 plain piping tube. Roll the remaining yellow piece into a sausage and push the end of a paintbrush into one end for the opening, then leave to dry. To make the bag, roll a ball of golden brown paste, then indent in the centre and pinch around the edge to shape. Cut out two circles for the handles using the piping tube and stretch them wider. Make the peas from the yellow-green trimmings, and stick in the bag and on the cake board using sugar glue.

DENNIS

5 Colour 60g (2oz) modelling paste red, 100g (3½oz) pale pink (using a tiny amount of red paste) and 75g (2½oz) black. Make Dennis's body using

30g (1oz) of red and stick on to the top of the cake. Split the remaining red in half and make Dennis's two sleeves. Push the end of a paintbrush into the bottom of each sleeve to indent, then stick in position using sugar glue. Using 60g (2oz) pale pink paste, make a ball nose and two ears, indenting the centre of each ear with a bone tool, then roll the remainder into a ball for his head and stick on to his body. Thinly roll out half the white modelling paste and cut out Dennis's eyes using the template on page 91. Stick in place with the nose and ears. Using the black modelling paste, model long teardrop shapes for his hair and stick in place. Roll very thin strips for his smile and eyebrows, make two flattened balls for his pupils and thinly roll out and cut strips for the stripes on his jumper. Assemble the peashooter, sticking with sugar glue. To make Dennis's hands, split 7g (¼oz) pale pink modelling paste exactly in half and follow the instructions on page 11. Stick each hand in place holding the peashooter in one hand and bag in the other.

GNASHER

6 Using the photograph as a guide, make Gnasher's head and ears from the remaining pale pink modelling paste. Use the no. 4 piping tube to dimple his smile in each corner. Roll two small balls of white modelling paste for his eyes and stick on to his face, pressing them flat and together. Roll out a tiny piece of white and cut a strip to fit his smile. Indent his teeth with a knife, then stick in place with sugar glue. Using the remaining black modelling paste, model a flattened piece for Gnasher's body, pinching around the edge. Assemble this with his head and ears on the cake next to Dennis. Model teardrop shapes for his hair, twisting up to a point, and stick over his head, then roll a ball for his nose and make his eyes and eyebrows.

Kipper

Cuddly Kipper the dog and his toys are great favourites with younger children.

Tip
Make sure the join in the sugarpaste behind Kipper's head is completely closed and smooth to prevent colour collecting in any imperfections when painting.

BOARD & CAKE

1 Roll out 500g (1lb) white sugarpaste and cover the cake board, trimming excess from the edge. Put aside to dry. Trim the crust from the round cake, keeping the rounded top where the cake has risen. Trim this into an oval-shaped cake by trimming 2.5cm (1 inch) from opposite sides of the cake, then trim around the base to taper in. Cut out a wedge at the front for the basket opening. Using the cake cuttings, build up the top of the cake.

Trim the crust from the two bowl-shaped cakes. Shape one to narrow the front and sides, and place on top of the other bowl cake, towards the back, to shape Kipper's head. The bottom bowl cake should protrude for the muzzle; trim this to shape a rounded muzzle. Cut a layer in the oval cake and sandwich back together using buttercream. Sandwich the two bowl cakes together using buttercream, then spread a thin layer over the surface of the cakes to help the sugarpaste stick. Position the cake on the cake board.

BASKET & BLANKET

2 Colour 470g (15oz) sugarpaste pale golden brown. Roll out and cut a strip measuring 60x7.5 cm (24x3 inches). Dust with icing sugar, then carefully roll up. Position the edge against the back of the cake, then unravel the strip of sugarpaste around the cake, smoothing the join closed. Trim out a piece of sugarpaste at the front for the basket opening.

Colour the royal icing pale golden brown. Using a no. 3 plain piping tube, pipe the basketweave effect around the cake, starting at the back. First pipe a vertical line from the top edge of the basket, then pipe three horizontal lines close together over this piped line, repeating three times down to the bottom. To continue, pipe another vertical line up against the horizontal lines, then pipe horizontal lines in sets of three in the gaps created. To give the basket a scruffy appearance, leave some of the piped lines broken. To finish, pipe a herringbone pattern around the base and top edge. Leave to dry.

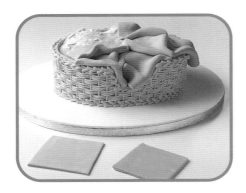

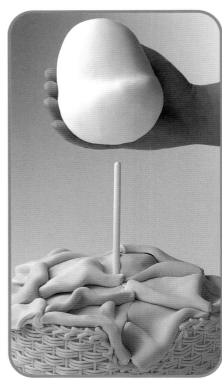

rounded. Flatten the rounded end slightly, then make a cut for the thumb. Move the thumb down slightly out of the way, then make two more cuts to make the fingers. Smooth the ridges to round off, and bend the hand slightly by pressing in the centre of the palm. Dilute some golden brown food colouring paste with water. Paint a thin coat of colour over Kipper's head and arm, leaving the muzzle and hand unpainted. Paint three thin coats, leaving to dry between each, keeping brush strokes to a minimum to prevent the previous coats from lifting. With a clean, damp paintbrush, blend in the edge around the muzzle and hand. Dilute a little dark brown food colouring paste with water to make a watery brown colourwash. Paint over the basket with a paintbrush, letting the colour go into the

3 Colour 140g (4½oz) sugarpaste pink and 140g (4½oz) green. Roll out each colour and cut into 7.5cm (3 inch) squares. Position over the top of the cake to create the checked blanket, tucking in the edges. Push the length of dowelling down into the centre of the cake.

KIPPER

4 Roll out 345g (11oz) white sugarpaste, lift and cover the front of Kipper's head, smoothing the sugarpaste around the back. Trim away any excess, then smooth the join closed. Lower Kipper's head down on to the dowelling, sticking the base to the blanket with sugar glue. Smooth at the front to encourage a little chin. To make Kipper's arm, roll 45g (1½oz) modelling paste into a sausage, keeping one end

gaps between the piped lines. Dilute some red food colouring and paint stripes over the checked blanket. Stick Kipper's arm in place.

RABBIT

5 Colour 45g (1½oz) modelling paste pale grey and 15g (½oz) pale pink. Using the photograph as a guide, model a teardrop

Tip
To hold Kipper's ears in place more securely, use sugar sticks (see page 11).

ing golden brown, model his eyes, then roll a long thin sausage and cut into strips for the blanket stitching. Using the remaining black, model Mr. Snake's pupils and Kipper's nose. Stick a strip of white paste along the join at the side of Mr. Snake for the opening, then roll two minute balls of white paste for the eye highlights.

HIPPO & FINISHING

8 Colour 60g (2oz) modelling paste dark pink. Roll a ball with half to make the hippo's body, then with the remaining piece model his head, two ears and four flattened balls for his feet. Assemble on the cake using sugar glue. To make Kipper's ears, first colour 45g (1½oz) modelling paste dark brown. Split into two and model two balls, pinching at either end to shape. Stick in place using sugar glue, and use foam pieces for support whilst drying. Dilute some red food colouring paste with water. Using a fine paintbrush, paint the flowers on the rabbit's bib. Stipple a tiny amount of palest red colour on to Kipper's muzzle. Dilute some black food colouring paste with water and, using the fine paintbrush, paint the fine lines for all the muzzles, eyes, eyebrows and the stitching on the side of Mr. Snake. Paint a little diluted golden brown on to Mr. Snake's eyes.

shape for the body, using half of the pale grey, and indent at the base using the end of a paintbrush for the legs to slot in. Using the remaining pale grey, roll a ball for the head and make two arms, two legs and two ears, indenting the centre of each ear with the end of a paintbrush. With a little white modelling paste, make the bib and muzzle. Using a little of the pale pink modelling paste, make the insides of the ears and a little oval-shaped nose. Stick in place with sugar glue. Assemble on the cake with the rabbit's hand tucked in Kipper's, using sugar glue to secure. Use pieces of foam for support whilst drying.

SLIPPER

6 To make the slipper, colour 100g (3½oz) modelling paste golden brown. Put aside enough to make the slipper's ears and Mr. Snake's eyes, then roll the remainder into a ball, then into an oval. Press in to indent and hollow out at one end, pinching around the edge. Roll two balls of paste for the ears, indenting in the centre of each using the large end of a bone tool. Stick in place using sugar glue. Colour 7g (¼oz) model-

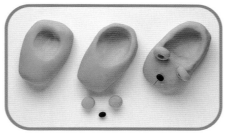

ling paste black. Using a minute amount, model a ball for the nose. Indent a line using the back of a knife, then stick the nose in place. Position the slipper on the cake using sugar glue to secure.

MR. SNAKE

7 To make Mr. Snake, colour 185g (6oz) modelling paste pale golden brown and 155g (5oz) pale blue. Put aside 7g (¼oz) of each colour for later, then roll sausage shapes with each colour measuring 23cm (9 inches) in length. Stick together with the pale golden brown on top. Press down along the edge to join. Position Mr. Snake on the cake board. Using the remaining blue and pink, model flattened pieces to decorate Mr. Snake's back. With the remain-

GARFIELD

Lovable, laid-back Garfield the cat enjoys a relaxed lifestyle. He is always happy to have a snack and a snooze.

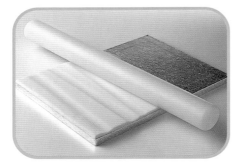

BOARD

1 Roll out 185g (6oz) sugarpaste and cover one half of the cake board. Indent by pressing down with the rolling pin to give a fabric effect, then put aside to dry.

GARFIELD'S BODY

2 Trim the crusts from the cakes, keeping rounded tops where the cakes have risen. Turn the cakes upside-down and position on the cake board. Spread the surface of both cakes with a layer of buttercream to help the sugarpaste stick.

3 Colour 1.17kg (2lb 5½oz) sugarpaste golden brown. Roll out 750g (1½lb) and cover the two cakes, smoothing the

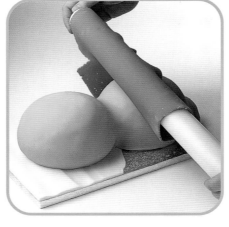

sugarpaste around the shapes and tucking under. To make the blanket, colour 315g (10oz) sugarpaste blue. Thinly roll out and cut a straight edge. Carefully lift the sugarpaste using the rolling pin. Position the sugarpaste with the straight edge at the back of Garfield's head, then apply the sugarpaste over his back and to the edge of the cake board, encouraging some pleats. Trim away excess, then secure with a little sugar glue.

GARFIELD'S FACE

4 Split 100g (3½oz) white sugarpaste in half and make the two oval shaped eyes. Cut a straight edge on the facing side of each eye so they stick together neatly, then stick in position on the cake. Colour a minute amount of sugarpaste black and make two tiny oval-shaped pupils. To make the mouth, colour 30g (1oz) sugarpaste pale golden brown and split into two. Roll both pieces into sausages, tapering one end of each to a rounded point. Pinch 2.5cm (1 inch) from the other end of each to shape rounded ends, bending around to

MATERIALS

two 1 litre (2 pint/5 cup) bowl-shaped cakes (see page 12)
30x20cm (12x8 inch) oblong cake board
1.825kg (3lb 10 ½ oz) sugarpaste (rolled fondant)
250g (8oz) buttercream
345g (11oz) pastillage
golden brown, blue, black, pink and brown food colouring pastes
sugar glue
cool boiled water

☆

EQUIPMENT

large rolling pin
sharp knife
cocktail sticks (toothpicks)
ruler
medium and fine paintbrushes

Tip

If preferred, you can split and fill each cake with buttercream, but only use a small amount so it doesn't add too much height to the finished cake.

shape the mouth corners, and pinch a tiny teardrop shape on the end of each. Stick in position, smoothing just under each eye to flatten slightly, then push the end of a paintbrush into the mouth corners to indent three times on either side. Colour 7g (¼oz) sugarpaste pale pink, make his oval-shaped nose and stick in place.

FRONT PAWS & EARS

6 Using 125g (4oz) golden brown sugarpaste for each, model Garfield's front paws. First roll a ball, then indent to round off the hands. Using the end of a paintbrush, indent to separate the fingers, then smooth out ridges. Stick in position against Garfield with the hands resting on the box edge. With 45g

(1½oz), make Garfield's ears, sticking in position pointing a little forwards.

GARFIELD'S TAIL

7 With the remaining golden brown sugarpaste, model Garfield's tail. Stick on to the cake using sugar glue, letting the tail curl over the box sides. Dilute black food colouring paste with some cool boiled water. Using the paintbrushes, paint Garfield's stripes.

THE BOX

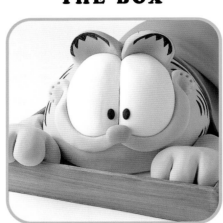

5 To make the box, roll out the pastillage and, using a ruler, cut strips to fit each side of the cake board, 4cm (1½ inches) in depth. Cover the two cake board ends first, then the two sides, smoothing the joins closed and sticking with sugar glue. Dilute a little brown food colouring paste with some cool boiled water. Using the medium paintbrush, paint a colourwash over the box. Keep the paintbrush a little dry to encourage streaking. Leave to dry for at least 8 hours, or overnight.

Like the Mr. Men, the Little Misses are colourful and full of fun.

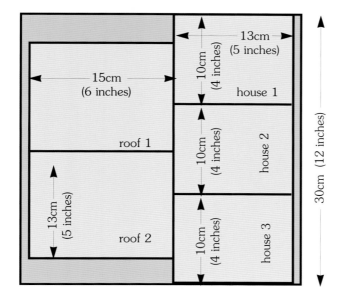

BOARD & CAKE

1 Colour 315g (10oz) sugarpaste green. Roll out and cover the cake board. Trim out a piece at the front of the cake board for the path. Colour 30g (1oz) sugarpaste brown. Roll out to the same thickness as the cake board covering and cut a path to fit the piece removed. Trim the crust from the cake and slice the top flat. Cut the cake as shown in the diagram. Put one of the two larger cakes on top of the other and trim to make the roof shape. Sandwich the layers together using buttercream. Sandwich the three smaller cakes together with

MATERIALS

30cm (12 inch) square cake (see page 13)
25cm (10 inch) petal-shaped cake board
1.5kg (3lb) sugarpaste (rolled fondant)
green, brown, yellow, red, black, blue, dark green, mauve, navy, pink and orange food colouring pastes
410g (13oz) buttercream
560g (1lb 2oz) modelling paste
sugar glue

EQUIPMENT

large and small rolling pins
sharp knife
2 cake smoothers
3cm (1¼ inch) and 1cm (½ inch) square cutters
piping tube (tip) or small circle cutter
small blossom plunger cutter
pieces of foam
fine paintbrush
black food colouring pen

MR.MEN   LITTLE MISS

buttercream to make the house. Spread a thin layer of buttercream over the surface of the cakes to help the sugarpaste stick.

HOUSE

2 Colour 750g (1½lb) sugarpaste yellow. Roll out a little at a time, positioning the house cake down on to it and cutting around. Cover the two sides first, then the back and front, smoothing the joins closed with a little sugar glue. Use cake smoothers to move the cake to prevent fingermarks. Position the cake on the cake board, lining up the centre front of the house with the path. Colour 315g (10oz) sugarpaste red. Roll out and cover the roof cake, smoothing the sugarpaste around the shape and a little under. Stick the roof cake in position on top of the house.

3 Cut four windows and a central door out of the front of the house using the 3cm (1¼ inch) square cutter, removing the sugarpaste.

Colour 15g (½oz) modelling paste black. Thinly roll out and cut four squares using the 3cm (1¼ inch) square cutter. Thinly roll out 15g (½oz) white modelling paste and cut four squares using the same cutter. Cut from each of these four 1cm (½ inch) squares to make the window frames. Stick in position on the black squares. Colour 90g (3oz) modelling paste blue and model eight small flattened balls. Use the piping tube to cut small semi-circle shapes, and stick in the windows for the curtains. Slot the windows into the front of the house. Using white modelling paste, roll out and cut the door frame. With blue modelling paste, make the door, four window-sills and the chimney, sticking with sugar glue.

TREE & BUSHES

4 To make the tree and bushes, colour 60g (2oz) modelling paste mid-green, 30g (1oz) dark green, 60g (2oz) yellow-green (using a little yellow and green food colouring paste), and 15g

(½oz) brown. To model a bush, roll a ball, flatten slightly, then cut three 'V's from one side. Smooth out the ridges to round off, then cut along the opposite side and at the bottom for the straight edges. Reserve a minute piece of mid-green modelling paste for Little Miss Naughty's bow, then make two mid-green bushes, one dark green bush, one yellow-green bush, a yellow-green flower-bed and a tree. Roll out the brown modelling paste and cut out a tree trunk. Stick the bushes in position against the side of the house and the tree against the back. Using the small blossom plunger cutter, make the flowers for the flower-bed using white modelling paste.

THE LITTLE MISSES

5 To make all the Little Misses, colour 45g (1½oz) modelling paste red, 30g (1oz) mauve, 22g (¾oz) blue, 45g (1½oz) yellow, 22g (¾oz) navy blue, 22g (¾oz) bright pink, 7g (¼oz) pale pink and 22g (¾oz) orange. Roll into balls of various

sizes. Model oval shapes for their feet, shaping some with legs. To make the two-tone shoes, make two oval shapes, one in blue and the other white. Slice each into three and stick alternate colours together. To make their hands, first model a tiny teardrop shape,

then twist the pointed end to form a wrist. Flatten the rounded end and make three cuts. Smooth the ridges to round off, then stick in position using pieces of foam for support whilst drying. To make the hats, model flattened circles for the

hat rims and small rounded domes for each top, trimming with thin strips of paste for the hat bands. The little bows are made by first modelling a tiny ball for the tie in the centre, then sticking on two triangular-shaped pieces to make the bow, indenting with a cocktail stick for the pleats if necessary. Make Little Miss Naughty's bow from the reserved mid-green paste, first making two small loops, then adding a short piece of paste on either side.

FINISHING

6 With the remaining red modelling paste, model pieces for the top of the front door, the door handle, the doorstep, flower centres and flattened balls for the tree. Leave the cake to dry completely for at least 8 hours, or overnight, then carefully draw in the Little Misses' features using a black food colouring pen.

Left to right on the cake board: Little Miss Fun, Little Miss Chatterbox, Little Miss Bossy, Little Miss Sunshine, Little Miss Twins, Little Miss Scatterbrain, Little Miss Shy. *At the window:* Little Miss Tiny. *On the roof:* Little Miss Naughty!

SONIC THE HEDGEHOG ™

Racing from one place to the next, barely stopping to catch his breath, Sonic is the fastest, coolest hedgehog – anywhere.

MATERIALS

3 litre (6 pint/13 cup) bowl-shaped cake (see page 12)
36cm (14 inch) round cake board
45g (1½ oz) pastillage
1.25kg (2½ lb) sugarpaste (rolled fondant)
470g (15oz) buttercream
375g (12oz) modelling paste
yellow, red, purple, white, blue, flesh, black and pink food colouring pastes
cool boiled water
yellow and gold dusting powders (petal dusts/blossom tints)
sugar stick (see page 11) or raw dried spaghetti
sugar glue

EQUIPMENT

large and small rolling pins
1cm (½ inch), 2cm (¾ inch), 7cm (2¾ inch) and 10cm (4 inch) circle cutters
ruler
cocktail sticks (toothpicks)
fine and medium paintbrushes
sharp knife
3cm (1¼ inch) square cutter
absorbent kitchen paper
pieces of foam
miniature star cutter
black food colouring pen

PASTILLAGE PIECES

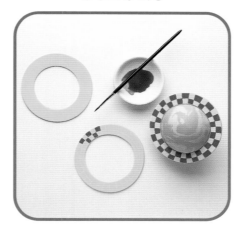

1 To allow plenty of drying time, make the pastillage planet ring and the golden rings first. Colour the pastillage yellow using yellow food colouring paste. Roll it out and cut out a large ring using 7cm (2¾ inch) and 10cm (4 inch) circle cutters. Roll out the trimmings, and cut four small rings using 1cm (½ inch) and 2cm (¾ inch) circle cutters. Using a ruler and cocktail stick, gently scratch the checks on the surface of the large ring. Dilute some red food colouring with a little water and paint the chequered effect over the large ring. Dust the small rings with gold dusting powder. Put all the rings aside to dry.

CAKE & BOARD

2 Colour 500g (1lb) sugarpaste pale purple and cover the cake board, trimming excess paste from around the edge. Paint different-sized white dots over the surface of the sugarpaste using white food colouring paste and a fine paintbrush, then set aside and leave to dry completely.

3 Trim the crust from the cake and slice the top flat. Cut two layers in the cake and sandwich back together using buttercream. Position on the cake board. Spread a thin layer of butter-

cream over the surface of the cake to help the sugarpaste stick.

4 Colour 375g (12oz) sugarpaste red. Using 375g (12oz) white and all the red sugarpaste, alternately roll out and cut squares using the 3cm (1¼ inch) square cutter. Position on the cake to create a chequered surface, trimming some of the squares to fit around the domed shape. Cover the surface of the cake completely. Protect the cake board with a sheet of absorbent paper. Using yellow dusting powder and a medium paintbrush, dust the cake yellow, fading out halfway round. Remove the absorbent paper.

SONIC

5 Colour 60g (2oz) modelling paste blue, 22g (¾oz) red, 7g (¼oz) flesh and a minute amount black. Using 7g (¼oz) of the blue for the body, legs and ears, roll a ball for his body, pinching two pointed prickles either side at the back. Stick in position on the cake. Roll two thin sausages for his legs, about 2.5cm (1 inch) long, bend and stick in position using a piece of foam to hold up the crossed-over leg while it dries. Model two triangular-shaped ears and put aside. Using sugar glue to secure, push a sugar

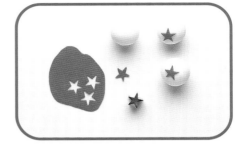

stick or piece of spaghetti down through the body, leaving about 2.5cm (1 inch) protruding from the top. Using 15g (½oz) blue modelling paste, first put a tiny piece aside for his eyebrows, then model Sonic's head using the photograph above as a guide for the prickles. Pinch each prickle to a point and bend round to curve downwards. Moisten the sugar stick or spaghetti with a little sugar glue, then carefully lower Sonic's head down on to it until his head touches his body. Stick his ears in place.

6 To make Sonic's shoes, model two pointed teardrop shapes from 7g (¼oz) red paste. Use 7g (¼oz) white paste for the shoe stripes, socks, gloves and eye area. Thinly roll out and cut two strips for his shoe stripes, then model four flattened balls and stick together in twos to make the socks. Indent the centre of each with the end of a paintbrush and, using sugar glue to secure, firmly slot in the two legs, again using some pieces of foam for support

while drying. Model two teardrop shapes for his gloves, flatten slightly and make cuts for the thumbs. Make three shorter cuts on each glove for the fingers and gently twist each finger to remove ridges and lengthen. Press in each palm to curve and shape. Stick two flattened balls together for each glove cuff, again indenting with the end of a paintbrush for the arms to slot in later. For the eye area, press two small oval balls of white paste flat, encouraging the bottom of each to touch. Stick on to Sonic's face with the bottom of the eye area exactly in the centre of his face. Using flesh modelling paste, model a flattened ball for his tummy, two triangular inner ears, his muzzle, and two thin arms. Using the tiny piece of blue modelling paste put aside, roll a thin sausage and stick above the white eye area, following the outline of his eyes. With the black modelling paste, model an oval nose and two tiny eyes. Stick everything in place, using foam pieces for support where necessary.

7 Using 15g (½oz) white modelling paste and the remaining red and blue, make three white balls, fifteen blue balls and six red balls, sticking in position with sugar glue. Thinly roll out some red modelling paste, cut out stars and stick on the white balls.

PLANETS

8 Colour 200g (6½oz) modelling paste pale blue and 30g (1oz) pink. To make the large ringed planet, put aside 7g (¼oz) pale blue modelling paste, then knead the pink modelling paste into the remainder until streaky. Roll into a smooth and crack-free ball large enough to hold the chequered pastillage ring made earlier. Stick on to the cake board with sugar glue. Knead the remaining white and blue modelling paste together until streaky, form into a smooth ball, and stick to the cake board for the small planet.

FINISHING

9 Carefully draw Sonic's smile using the black food colouring pen. Stick the gold rings in position over the cake.

MATERIALS

20cm (8 inch) and 15cm (6 inch)
round cakes (see page 12)
30cm (12 inch) round cake board
440g (14oz) buttercream
1.25kg (2½lb) sugarpaste (rolled
fondant)
185g (6oz) modelling paste
brown, green, red, yellow, golden
brown, pink, mauve, blue and black
food colouring pastes
cool boiled water
sugar glue

EQUIPMENT

sharp knife
large and small rolling pins
medium firm bristle paintbrush
medium and fine paintbrushes
absorbent kitchen paper
cocktail sticks (toothpicks)
small, medium and large
ivy leaf cutters
small leaf veiner
bone tool
small double curve serrated crimping
tool
small primrose cutter
pieces of foam
2cm (¾ inch) circle cutter
blossom plunger cutter

BRAMBLY HEDGE

Inspired by the well-loved tales of Brambly Hedge, children will be delighted with this enchanting scene.

CAKE & BOARD

1 Trim the crust from each cake and slice the tops flat. Cut both cakes horizontally in half, then reassemble and position the small cake on top of the large cake, slightly off centre. Shape the tree trunk by slicing down from the top, all the way around, sloping outwards and down to about 2.5cm (1 inch) above the base. Position the cake on the cake board.

Trim out pieces of cake for the front and back doorways. Trim out a smaller doorway on each side. To make the base of the cake wider, position some of the trimmings around the base and trim again, sloping out down to the cake board and making an uneven edge. Using buttercream, sandwich the layers together, then spread a thin layer over the surface of the cake to help the sugarpaste stick.

2 Roll out 875g (1¾lb) sugarpaste and cover the cake completely, stretching out the pleats and smoothing downwards. If there is a pleat that can't be smoothed out, cut away and smooth the join closed with your hands. Trim excess from around the base, trimming into each doorway. Pinch around the top edge to create a ridge. Make four window recesses by indenting with your finger. Mark vertical lines and ridges with a knife and paintbrush handle.

To make the large branch, roll 140g (4½oz) sugarpaste into a sausage about 20cm (8 inches) long. Separate one end into two branches. Twist each branch to lengthen and narrow to a point. Cut the end of one branch to separate again, twisting to a point.

Using sugar glue, stick the branch in position, curving it around from the top of the cake over the top of the front door recess, down to the cake board. Make a smaller branch, using 90g (3oz) sugarpaste, and stick on the side of the cake, curving it over the top of the side door recess. Mark lines on the branches with a knife.

HOUSE

3 Dilute some brown food colouring paste with cool boiled water until quite pale. Using the firm bristle paintbrush, paint a brown wash over the surface of the cake. To represent the moss and bark on the trunk, separately dilute some brown and green food colouring pastes with a little less water for stronger colours. Remove excess colour from the paintbrush by dabbing on absorbent paper, then paint green and brown horizontal and vertical brushstrokes over the cake, leaving the top unpainted. Paint some brown into each window recess.

Roll the remaining sugarpaste into a strip and use to cover the cake board, butting it up against the tree trunk and around the branches, pushing the sugarpaste into each doorway. Press with your fingers to make the surface uneven, then trim excess from around the cake board edge.

Paint the stippled effect over the cake board using diluted green and brown. Paint grass at the base of the tree trunk using the diluted green and a fine paintbrush. Mix a little brown into some of the green to change the shade and stipple on some more. Leave to dry, then, using the fine paintbrush, paint flowers on the board using diluted red colouring.

Thinly roll out 22g (¾oz) modelling

paste and cut out five different-sized doors, one for each recess and one for just above the smaller branch. Mark lines on each using the back of a knife. To make each door handle, roll tiny balls of paste, again in different sizes, and indent in the centre of each with a cocktail stick. To make the windows, roll out 15g (½oz) modelling paste and cut strips. Stick over each window recess, building up the frame first, then adding tiny strips for the panes. Make two arched and two square windows. Roll out 22g (¾oz) modelling paste and cut out 27–30 ivy leaves in different sizes, shaping them in the leaf veiner as each one is cut. Stick in position on the side of the cake. Using the modelling paste trimmings, model the chimney for the side of the cake, sticking in place with sugar glue. Paint two different shades of green over the ivy leaves. Mix a darker shade of brown and paint all the windows and doors, and the chimney. Paint a pale yellow wash over the top of the cake.

PICNIC & APPLES

4 To make the picnic cloth for the top of the cake, thinly roll out 7g (¼oz) modelling paste and cut a square to fit. Position on the cake, encouraging some pleats. Model the trimmings into four small circles of paste for the jam tarts and indent the centre of each with the large end of a bone tool. To make the cheese, model a flattened circle of modelling paste using 7g (¼oz), and cut out a wedge. Push the end of a paintbrush into the paste repeatedly to create holes. Use 7g (¼oz) modelling paste to make the apples. First make five tiny apple stalks. Split the remaining piece into five and roll into balls that taper in at the base. Indent the top using the end of a paintbrush, and stick the stalks in place.

BASKET & FLOWERS

5 Make the basket using 7g (¼oz) modelling paste. First roll a thin sausage of paste, fold it over and twist into a handle. Trim the ends and set aside for a few moments to dry. Roll a ball with the remaining piece and crimp around the sides and top edge with the crimping tool. To make holes for the handle to sit in, press the end of a paintbrush into the top of the basket on either side. Using sugar glue, slot the handle in place. To make the primroses and primrose leaves, thinly roll out 15g (½oz) modelling paste and cut out eight flowers and two leaf shapes. Indent the centre of each flower using the large end of the bone tool and carefully fold each leaf in half to mark the veins. Stick in position on the side of the cake. Shape the trimmings into three strawberry shapes, mark the surface and top of each with a cocktail stick, and place in the basket.

PRIMROSE

6 Each Brambly Hedge mouse is made from 7g (¼oz) white modelling paste. They all have very rounded bodies with teardrop-shaped heads which turn up slightly at the nose. To make Primrose (the girl mouse dancing at the front), first

model a teardrop shape for her dress, pinching around the base to shape. For the sleeves, model long tear-drop shapes, marking pleats with a cocktail stick. Using the end of a paintbrush, indent the point of each sleeve so the hands will slot in. As each piece is modelled, stick in place using sugar glue. Use foam pieces for support while drying.

Model a rounded teardrop for Primrose's head, turning up the muzzle slightly by tapping gently underneath with your finger. Mark her smile using the circle cutter just under the muzzle. Thinly roll out some paste and cut out a circle with the circle cutter for her hat brim. Model a dome-shaped piece of paste and stick it on top. Model flattened teardrop shapes for her feet and hands, making three cuts in each. Model a minute nose and stick high on the end of her muzzle. For her ears, model tiny teardrop shapes and indent each using the small end of the bone tool. Roll a long thin tapering tail and stick in place, twisting into a curl. Make her pinafore by modelling a flattened teardrop, and cut off the point for the top. Mark some pleats using a cocktail stick. Thinly roll out and cut strips for the back of the pinafore, looping into a bow, and a strip for her hat ribbon. Using a blossom plunger cutter, make six tiny blossoms for her hat.

BASIL

7 To make Basil (the sleeping mouse), model rounded teardrop shapes for his body and head. Open up his mouth with the end of a paint-brush and shape into a smile with a cocktail stick. Thinly roll out and cut a strip for his jacket and stick it

around the top half of his body. Model two little sleeves, indenting the end of each as for Primrose's sleeves. Stick Basil's head in place. Cut out a tiny square of paste for the bottom of his suit and roll three balls of paste, one each for the tops of his legs and tail, pressing the end of a paintbrush into each to indent a hole for the legs and tail to slot in. Make the ears, nose, hands, feet and tail as for Primrose, but twist up at the point of each teardrop-shaped foot to create his little legs.

WILFRED

8 To make Wilfred (the dancing boy mouse), model a ball for the bottom half of his body and shape his top, hollowing out the base to sit over the body. Make two sleeves as for Primrose, marking pleats with a cocktail stick. Make a small circle of paste, indented in the centre as before, to help hold his raised foot in place. Make the head, nose, ears, hands, feet and tail as before.

MR APPLE

10 Make Mr Apple in the same way as Wilfred, but with his feet slotted underneath in a standing position. Place an apple in his arms, securing it with sugar glue.

MRS APPLE

9 Make Mrs Apple (with strawberry basket) in the same way as Primrose, but without a hat, sticking the basket against her dress with her hands holding the handle.

MR AND MRS TOADFLAX

11 To make Mr and Mrs Toadflax (the picnicking mice), model Mrs Toadflax like Primrose, turning her feet so the undersides show as she is in a sitting position. Make Mr Toadflax like Wilfred, but with balls of paste indented as before to hold the feet and tail. Place a jam tart in his hands up against his mouth and model a little napkin tucked under his chin. Secure with sugar glue.

PAINTING

12 Before you start painting the mice and other features on the cake, refer to the section on painting on pages 10–11.

BANANAS IN PYJAMAS

TM

MATERIALS

30cm (12 inch) square cake (see page 13)
36cm (14 inch) oval cake board
2.85kg (5¾lb) sugarpaste (rolled fondant)
500g (1lb) buttercream
green, yellow, blue, golden brown and black food colouring pastes
sugar glue

☆

EQUIPMENT

sharp knife
10cm (4 inch), 9cm (3½ inch) and 7.5cm (3 inch) circle cutters
large rolling pin
black and dark blue food colouring pens

Tip

Make sure B1 and B2 are well balanced when buttercreaming the layers together. This will help prevent them leaning as they dry.

The charm of B1 and B2 is easy to see; children just go bananas over them. They look the same and think the same, so of course they both want to be the highlight of the party.

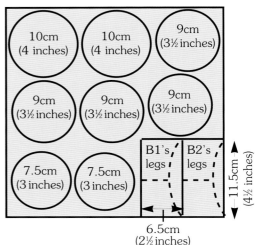

CAKE & BOARD

1 Colour 500g (1lb) sugarpaste green. Roll out and cover the cake board, then put aside to dry. Trim the crust from the cake and slice the top flat. Cut the cake as shown in the cutting diagram, using a sharp knife and circle cutters. Each banana has four layers and a separate piece for the legs. Assemble each cake with the 10cm (4 inch) circle of cake at the bottom, using two 9cm (3½ inch) circles for the second and third layers and a 7.5cm (3 inch) circle for the top, positioning the top layer slightly towards the back. To shape B1, slice down from the top all the way round to remove the ridges. Using the photograph as a guide, shape the cake by slicing a curve at the back and rounding off the top. Trim the legs as shown in the photograph and by

the dotted lines on the diagram, trimming a wedge from the top to separate them, and rounding off the sides. Repeat the procedure for B2.

2 Using buttercream, sandwich the cake layers together, then spread a thin layer over the surface of the cakes to help the sugarpaste stick. Position B1 on the cake board. Roll 140g (4½oz)

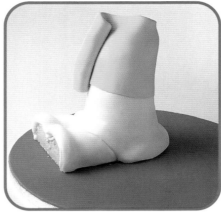

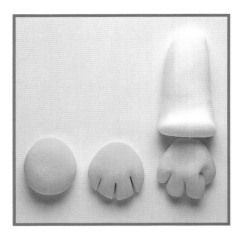

sugarpaste into a long sausage and use to edge the bottom of the legs and around the base of the pyjama top on both B1 and B2. Press the sausage flatter at the side of both pyjamas where B1 and B2 will be pushed together.

cake board as close to B2 as possible, then carefully pick up B2 with both hands, holding the sides and supporting the back, and position him as quickly as you can on the board beside B1, with their heads just touching.

HANDS & SLEEVES

5 Using the photograph above as a guide, model a flattened ball from 30g (1oz) yellow sugarpaste. Make a cut

COVERING

3 Roll out 375g (12oz) sugarpaste and cover B1's legs and up to the bottom of the second cake layer for his pyjamas, smoothing the sugarpaste around the back. Trim and smooth the join closed and trim excess from around the base. Using the back of a knife, indent around the bottom of the pyjama top to make it look like it is tucked under. Repeat for B2. Reserve the sugarpaste trimmings.

4 Colour 500g (1lb) sugarpaste yellow. Roll out 185g (6oz) and cut a strip to cover the top of B1. Loosely roll up and, starting at the back, unravel around the cake, smoothing the join closed. Repeat for B2. Reserve the trimmings. Bring the

for the thumb, then two smaller cuts for the fingers. Shape the hand by smoothing the ridges and rounding off the top of the thumb and each finger, then indent the palm by pressing in the centre. Using 90g (3oz), make three more hands and stick in position on the cake board up against the pyjama legs. Split 315g (10oz) white sugarpaste in four and model the sleeves, pinching at the base of each to create the fullness, then stick in place. Colour 155g (5oz) sugarpaste blue. Thinly roll out and cut strips, and stick them one at a time over the pyjamas to create the striped effect.

SHOES

6 Split 375g (12oz) sugarpaste into four. Model oval shapes and flatten slightly, narrowing at each heel. Roll out another 100g (3½oz), and cut out four soles using the templates on page 91.

Smooth around the edges to round off. Thinly roll out some yellow sugarpaste trimmings and cut out the shoe bands, using the templates on page 91. Stick in place with sugar glue. Roll four small balls of white sugarpaste for the shoe buttons. Moisten the bottoms of the trousers with sugar glue, then press each shoe in position, holding for a few moments until secure. Using white sugarpaste trimmings and the template on page 91, cut out the collars and model six buttons for the pyjamas. Stick in position.

FINISHING

7 Colour 7g (¼oz) sugarpaste dark golden brown. Model the two stalks and stick in position with a little sugar glue. Leave the cake to dry, then with the black food colouring pen, draw in the eyes and smiles. Write 'B1' and 'B2' on their respective collars using the dark blue food colouring pen. With a minute amount of the remaining white sugarpaste, model a tiny highlight for each eye.

MATERIALS

1 litre (2 pint/5 cup) and 750ml
(1¼ pint/3 cup) bowl-shaped cakes
(see page 13)
30cm (12 inch) round cake board
2kg (4lb) sugarpaste (rolled fondant)
315g (10oz) buttercream
blue, red, cream, yellow, brown and
black food colouring pastes
sugar glue

EQUIPMENT

large rolling pin
sharp knife
13cm (5 inch) and 18cm (7 inch)
circle cutters
plastic dowelling
paintbrush
pieces of foam

Tip

Don't be tempted to cut
layers in the cakes and fill
with buttercream. The weight
of the stacked cakes will push
the buttercream out and
cause bulges.

SUPER MARIO 64

®

Anyone keen on computer games will know Mario, the fun-loving Italian plumber from Nintendo. Present this cake with golden coins scattered on the party table and you're sure to score lots of points.

CAKES & BOARD

1 Colour 375g (12oz) sugarpaste pale blue. Roll out and cover the cake board, then put aside to dry. Trim the crusts from the two cakes, keeping the top of each rounded where it has risen. Trim a wedge from one side of the large cake to flatten Mario's tummy area, and position the cake on the board, near the front. To shape the smaller cake for Mario's head, trim the rounded base slightly for Mario's face (the risen area of the cake will be the back of his head). Cut a small wedge from the neck area so the small cake will sit comfortably on the large cake. Spread a thin layer of buttercream over the surface of both cakes to help the sugarpaste stick.

HEAD

2 Colour 440g (14oz) sugarpaste red. Roll out 90g (3oz) and cut a circle using the 13cm (5 inch) circle cutter. Position the circle on top of the body, smoothing down at the front. Colour 185g (6oz) sugarpaste cream. Using 15g (½ oz), pad the facial features as shown in the photograph, below, by rolling two balls and pressing them flatter for his cheeks, shaping a piece to make his lips fuller, and rolling a sausage that tapers into points at each end to form his chin and jaw. Roll out 90g (3oz) cream sugarpaste and cut a circle using the 13cm (5 inch) circle cutter. To make the circle wider to stretch around the sides of Mario's face, roll over the circle using the

rolling pin to make a more oval shape. Position over the face, smoothing around the facial padding.

OVERALLS

4 To make the overalls, first colour 580g (1lb 2½oz) sugarpaste blue. Using 170g (5½oz), split it into two and make two fat sausage shapes for the trouser legs. Stick on the cake board up against the back of the cake. Roll out 410g (13oz) and cut a strip 45x10cm (18x5 inches). Loosely roll up both ends to meet in the centre. Position the centre against the front of Mario with the top edge meeting the red, then unravel around his body, smoothing around the back and

over the legs. Trim away excess, reserving the trimmings. Smooth the join closed and trim around the base. Pinch around the bottom of the trouser legs to widen and pinch up. Using the trimmings and the braces template on page 93, cut out two braces and stick in position using sugar glue. Reserve the blue trimmings. Colour 7g (¼oz) sugarpaste dark yellow and model the two buttons for the braces, sticking in place with sugar glue.

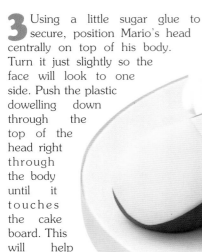

3 Using a little sugar glue to secure, position Mario's head centrally on top of his body. Turn it just slightly so the face will look to one side. Push the plastic dowelling down through the top of the head right through the body until it touches the cake board. This will help support the cake and hold the head in place.

SHOES

5 Colour 250g (8oz) sugarpaste brown. Using 200g (6½oz), make the shoes. Split the paste in half and model two oval shapes. Roll one end of each to narrow the heels. Roll out 22g (¾oz) cream sugarpaste and cut out two soles using the template on page 93. Mark the heels with a knife and stick on to the shoes with sugar glue. Stick the shoes in position, pressing the heels against the trouser legs.

ARMS, GLOVES & HAT WINGS

6 To make the arms, split 100g (3½oz) red sugarpaste in half, roll the pieces into sausage shapes and flatten them slightly. Cut off one end of each to give a straight edge at the cuff. Stick the sleeves to the sides of the cake. Split 75g (2½oz) white sugarpaste in half and make the two gloves, using the photograph below as a guide. Stick the gloves to the sleeves and against the cake. Using 7g (¼oz) white paste, roll two sausages for the cuffs and stick over the joins to secure the arms and gloves together. Use foam pieces to support each arm whilst drying. To make the hat wings, split 45g (1½oz) white sugarpaste in two and model two

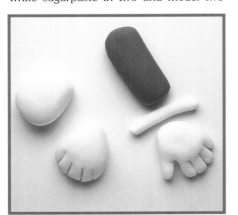

flattened teardrops. Indent along each one with the back of a knife, pushing in at the ends to scallop. Bend each to curve slightly and put aside to dry.

HAT & FEATURES

7 To make Mario's hat, first pad out the top of his head by rolling a sausage using 45g (1½oz) red sugarpaste, tapering the two ends to a point. Stick this above Mario's forehead, pinching up the centre. Roll out 185g (6oz) red paste and cut a circle using the 18cm (7 inch) circle cutter. Roll the circle into a more oval shape and position on top of the head over the hat padding, positioning the oval lengthways from the top to the bottom of the hat. Shape the hat, tuck-

ing under the cut edge around the back and pinching to round off. With the red trimmings and the template on page 93, roll out and cut the hat peak (visor). Stick in place, smoothing upwards as it sets. Stick the hat wings in place and use foam pieces for support while they dry. Using the remaining brown sugarpaste, model flattened pieces for Mario's hair at the back, pinching up curls at the ends, and small teardrop shapes for his sideburns. With the remaining white sugarpaste and the templates on page 93, thinly roll out and cut the hat badge and two eyes, sticking in place with sugar glue. Thinly roll out some red trimmings and cut out the letter 'M' for his hat badge using the template. Knead a little of the remaining white sugarpaste with some blue trimmings to make a slightly lighter blue for his eyes. Thinly roll out and cut the two blue irises using the template on page 93. Colour 15g (½oz) sugarpaste black. Using the templates, thinly roll out and cut a moustache, pupils and eyebrows, sticking in position with sugar glue. With 30g (1oz) cream sugarpaste, roll a ball for the nose and stick in place, then make two ears with the remaining cream, indenting the centre of each with your finger. Stick a minute ball of white sugarpaste on each eye to highlight.

MATERIALS

25cm (10 inch) square cake (see page 12)
36cm (14 inch) square cake board
1.6kg (3¼ lb) modelling paste
1.375kg (2¾lb) sugarpaste (rolled fondant)
500g (1lb) buttercream
green, golden brown, orange, brown, blue, yellow and black food colouring pastes
cool boiled water
sugar glue
sugar sticks (see page 11) or length of raw dried spaghetti

☆

EQUIPMENT

large and small rolling pins
sharp knife
2.5cm (1 inch), 3cm (1¼ inch) and 5cm (2 inch) square cutters
2cm (¾ inch) and 3cm (1¼ inch) circle cutters
cake smoother
18cm (7 inch) wooden dowelling
fine and medium paintbrushes
miniature circle cutter
small shell piping tube (tip)
cocktail sticks (toothpicks)
bone tool
pieces of foam

 Tip To simplify this cake, you could make just one armchair with modelled figure and present it on a smaller cake board.

Wallace & Gromit ™

TEA-TIME SCENE

Here are Wallace & Gromit, everyone's favourite duo, in a typical living-room scene. Anyone for a nice cup of tea and cheese and biscuits? Wensleydale, of course.

BOARD

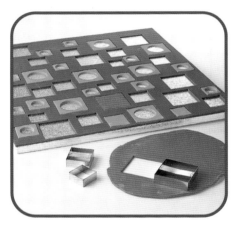

1 Colour 500g (1lb) modelling paste green and 140g (4½oz) pale golden brown. Colour 155g (5oz) modelling paste dark orange using orange colouring with a little brown, and 280g (9oz) cream using a touch of the golden brown. Roll out all the green paste and cover the cake board. With the square cutters, cut and remove different-sized squares. Reserve the trimmings. Roll out the pale golden brown and cut squares to fill half of the spaces. Slot in position, then, using the circle cutters, cut and remove circles from the golden brown squares. Reserve the trimmings. Roll out the dark orange modelling paste and cut different-sized squares to fill the remaining spaces. Cut and remove circles as before, reserving the trimmings. Roll out 100g (3½oz) of the cream modelling paste and cut different-sized circles to fill the spaces. For a smooth surface and to close any gaps, rub over the surface of the cake board with a cake smoother, then set aside to dry.

LAMP

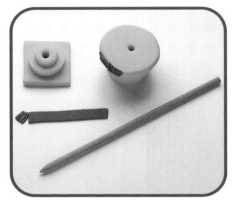

2 Colour 125g (4oz) modelling paste dark cream using golden brown food colouring. Using 90g (3oz), shape the lampshade, indenting the top a little. Thickly roll out the remaining piece and cut a 5cm (2 inch) square and two circles, 2cm (¾ inch) and 3cm (1¼ inches). Stick the two circles on top of the square using sugar glue. Press the dowelling into the centre of the lampshade to a depth of no more than 1cm (½ inch) and remove, then push into the lamp base right through to the bottom, and remove, to make support holes for when the lampshade is assembled later. Thinly roll out a strip of green modelling paste trimmings. To make the lampshade frill, make little cuts in groups of five or six and stick each piece against the edge of the lampshade as soon as it is made. Dilute some brown food colouring paste with a little water. Using the medium paintbrush, paint a wash of brown over the lamp base and dowelling. Roll out the dark cream trimmings and cut little strips for the straw that Shaun the sheep is eating. Put everything aside to dry.

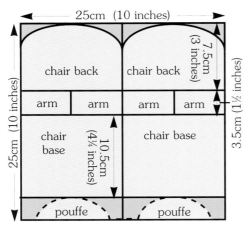

25cm (10 inches)

chair back · chair back

7.5cm (3 inches)

arm · arm · arm · arm

3.5cm (1½ inches)

chair base · chair base

25cm (10 inches)

10.5cm (4¼ inches)

pouffe · pouffe

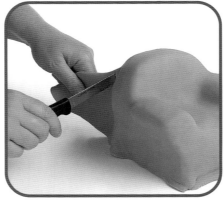

ARMCHAIRS

3 Trim the crust from the cake, slice the top flat and cut as shown in the diagram. To assemble an armchair, first trim a 1cm (½ inch) layer from the chair back. Put the chair back on top of the chair base, then position the two arm pieces. Trim the ridges from the top to round off, move each arm out slightly to widen the seat, then trim downwards from the outside so the arms are in line with the chair base. With the 1cm (½ inch) layer cut from the chair back, trim a seat cushion to fit between the two arms. Repeat for the second armchair. With the remaining pieces of cake, shape a circle for the pouffe, trimming the edge to round off and padding out with trimmings if required. Sandwich all layers together using buttercream, then spread a thin layer of buttercream over the surface of each cake to help the sugarpaste stick.

4 To cover the blue armchair, first colour 750g (1½ lb) sugarpaste blue and 45g (1½oz) modelling paste yellow. Roll out 625g (1¼lb) of the blue sugarpaste, lift carefully with the large rolling pin and position over the cake. Smooth around the shape with your hands, pulling up a pleat at the back. Trim this pleat away and smooth the join closed. Trim excess from around the base and

position the chair on the cake board. Use the cake smoother to create a smooth surface. Mark a line to separate the seat cushion at the front of the armchair using the back of a knife. Colour 625g (1¼lb) sugarpaste dark orange as before and use to cover the second armchair. Position on the board and mark the seat cushion as before. Using the end of a paintbrush, press in to indent little dots in triangular groups over the surface of the dark orange armchair. Roll out the remaining blue sugarpaste and cover the pouffe, smoothing the sugarpaste around and underneath. Press in near the top to indent a hole for the straw. Using 15g (½oz) yellow modelling paste and some of the green trimmings, roll thin sausages of paste and use for the edging on the armchairs and pouffe, then thinly roll out and cut little yellow circles using the miniature circle cutter and stick over the surface of the blue armchair and pouffe using sugar glue. Reserve the trimmings.

SHAUN THE SHEEP

5 First colour 140g (4½oz) modelling paste ivory using a minute amount of golden brown colouring, and colour 75g (2½oz) black. Model an oval body using

45g (1½oz) ivory, then, with 15g (½oz) make Shaun's tail, eyes and the top of his head. Texture the fleece by repeatedly pressing the tip of the shell piping tube into the paste. With 15g (½oz) black modelling paste, model his head, ears, four legs and pupils, sticking each piece in place as soon as it is made, assembling on the cake board. Make a hole in each pupil by pressing in the tip of a cocktail stick. Stick the straw in place, bursting out of a hole in the pouffe, and position some at Shaun's mouth.

GROMIT

6 Using some green and dark orange trimmings, make the two cushions for Gromit's chair, weighing 30g (1oz) each, and stick in place with a little sugar glue. To make Gromit, first model a teardrop shape for his body using 45g (1½oz) cream modelling paste. Twist the point of the teardrop to shape a neck. Stick on the chair, quite near the back, resting against the cushions. To help sup-

then make cuts for the thumbs and fingers. Shape the finger and thumb and bend the arms at the elbows. Stick in position and support with pieces of foam while drying. Colour 100g (3½oz) modelling paste brown. Using a little for each, make Gromit's two ears and stick in place, again using foam pieces for support whilst drying. With a minute amount of ivory and black, make his nose and eyes, indenting the centre of each pupil as before. To make the newspaper, thinly roll out 30g (1oz) ivory modelling paste and cut two oblongs measuring 10x6cm (4x2½ inches). Stick one on top of the other. Fold in half, then open and stick in Gromit's hands.

WALLACE

7 To make Wallace, model the remaining brown modelling paste into a flattened sausage and cut down three-quarters of its length to separate the legs. Smooth out the ridges and flatten the bottom of each leg. Stick to the seat of the dark orange armchair with the bottom of each leg on Shaun's back, using foam to support the legs. With 30g (1oz) yellow and some of the remaining golden

brown trimmings, make the two cushions, sticking them on either side of the armchair. With 60g (2oz) green trimmings, model Wallace's pullover, pressing in a small 'V' at the neck using the tip of a knife. To give the pullover a knitted look, mark lines across using a knife, and indent a herring-bone pattern between the lines with a cocktail stick. Position over the top of the trousers and stick with sugar glue.

For Wallace's arms, split 30g (1oz) ivory modelling paste in half and model two sleeves, bending each halfway along for the elbows, and marking creases on the insides with a cocktail stick. Press the end of a paintbrush into the end of each sleeve to indent so the hands will slot in easily. Stick in position, pressing at the shoulder to flatten a little. With a little ivory modelling paste, fill the 'V' level to the shoulder. Make Wallace's hands (see page 11) using 7g (¼oz) cream modelling paste split in two.

Using the photograph below as a guide, make Wallace's head, nose and ears with 45g (1½oz) cream modelling paste. Use the large end of a bone tool to indent the eye sockets and hollow out the mouth. Make his nose and ears, indenting the centre of each ear with the small end of the bone tool. Roll out a tiny amount of ivory coloured modelling paste and cut two thin strips. Indent along each with the back of a knife to mark his teeth. Moisten his mouth with sugar glue, then carefully slot the teeth in place. Model two eyes as before. Push a sugar stick into Wallace's body as before, moisten with sugar glue, then lower Wallace's head down on to it. Thinly roll out a little of the remaining ivory modelling paste and cut a strip for his collar. Moisten with sugar glue and wrap around his neck, joining the top at the front. With a little of the remaining dark orange modelling paste, make his tie. Using the remaining cream modelling paste, make

port the head, insert a sugar stick into the neck, leaving about 2.5cm (1 inch) protruding. With 30g (1oz) cream paste, model his head by rolling a ball, then pinch at the top to shape his eye and forehead area. Indent the underneath with a bone tool to create a hole for the neck to slot in easily. Moisten the sugar stick with sugar glue and lower Gromit's head down on to it. Using the large end of a bone tool, indent the eye sockets. To make the legs, split a 15g (½oz) piece of cream modelling paste in half. Roll sausages and indent at one end all the way round to shape ankles. Round off the feet, make two cuts at the end of each and shape the toes. Pinch at the back to shape the heels. Stick in position against Gromit's body, dangling over the front of the chair. To make the arms, split another 15g (½oz) cream modelling paste in half. Roll sausages and again indent at the end for the wrists and round off the hands. Press the hands a little flat,

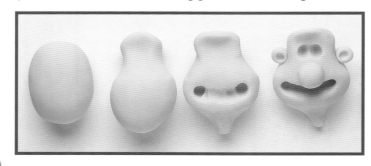

his slippers: model an oval and pinch up a flap at the front. Shape a flattened piece for the sole and stick to the base, indenting a line for the heel with a knife. Make the other slipper and stick both in position on Shaun's back, up against the bottom of Wallace's trouser legs.

PIGGY BANK

8 To make the piggy bank, colour 30g (1oz) modelling paste peach using a touch of orange colouring.

Model a ball, then shape a muzzle, indenting the end by pressing in gently with your finger. Push the end of a paintbrush into the muzzle to mark the nostrils. For the slot, press in the tip of a knife. To make the feet, shape four small teardrops and position them with the points inwards, moisten with sugar glue, then lower the piggy bank down on to them. Model two ears, indenting the centre of each with the small end of the bone tool, and stick in position pointing upwards. For the tail, roll a sausage and stick in place curling round. Make two tiny ivory eyes, indenting the centre of each with a cocktail stick. Position the piggy bank on the cake board, securing with sugar glue.

FINISHING

9 Roll out the remaining dark orange modelling paste and cut an oblong for the tray. Leave to dry on a flat surface. With the dark orange and green trimmings, roll a thin sausage of each colour, moisten with sugar glue along their length, then twist together to make the tray edging. Stick in place.

To make the saucer and small plate, roll out a little of the remaining green modelling paste and blue sugarpaste, and cut out two circles using the 3cm (1¼ inch) circle cutter. To shape them, place both on a piece of foam and indent in the centre with the smaller circle cutter. Model a little green cup and handle, hollowing the cup out using the bone tool, then pinching around the top to thin. Make the teapot with the remaining black modelling paste: roll a ball and indent the top with the small circle cutter to mark the lid. Model a ball for the lid handle and roll a sausage for the teapot handle. Shape the spout and indent the end with the end of a paintbrush.

With the golden brown and yellow trimmings, make the crackers and cheese, indenting the surface of each cracker by pressing the tip of a cocktail stick over it. Stick everything in place using sugar glue. Separately dilute some black, orange and green food colouring paste with a little water. Using the fine paintbrush, paint the print on the newspaper, the checked slippers and the flowers and leaves over the carpet and lampshade. Assemble the lampshade, sticking to the cake board to secure.

MATERIALS

30cm (12 inch) square cake (see page 13)
25cm (10 inch) square cake board
1.75kg (3½lb) sugarpaste (rolled fondant)
440g (14oz) buttercream
black, brown, blue, cream and green food colouring pastes
cool boiled water
sugar glue
1 teaspoon clear piping gel

☆

EQUIPMENT

large rolling pin
sharp knife
ruler
cocktail sticks (toothpicks)
absorbent kitchen paper
large firm bristle paintbrush
bone tool
black food colouring pen

To help prevent runs when painting the cake, keep the brush only just moist, and brush from the base of the cake upwards.

Wallace & Gromit ™

GROMIT

Gromit in his kennel, a quick and easy version for Wallace & Gromit fans, but still eye-catching and adorable.

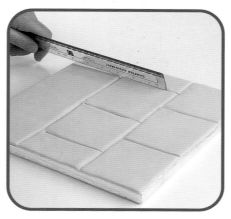

BOARD

1 Colour 375g (12oz) sugarpaste stone using a touch each of the black and brown food colouring pastes. Roll out and cover the cake board. Press the ruler edge into the paste to mark the paving, smoothing along the lines with your fingers to round off sharp edges. Press over the surface with your hands to make the surface uneven, then put aside to dry.

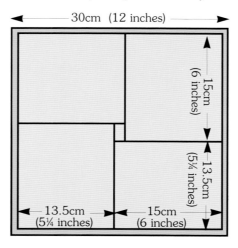

CAKE

2 Trim the crust from the cake, slice the top flat and cut as in the diagram. Pile the cakes one on top of the other. To shape the roof, trim from the centre of the top down one side at an outward angle, cutting down through two layers. Repeat for the opposite side. Sandwich all the layers together using buttercream, then spread a thin layer over the surface of the cake to help the sugarpaste stick. Position the cake on the cake board.

KENNEL

3 Measure the back of the kennel. Roll out 200g (6½oz) white sugarpaste and indent the lines for the wood planks by pressing the ruler edge into the surface. Using your measurements, cut out the shape of the back of the kennel. Mark the woodgrain effect with a knife. Lift carefully and position against the back of the kennel. Cover the sides and the front in the same way using 440g (14oz) sugarpaste. To represent the

(Diagram)
30cm (12 inches)
15cm (6 inches)
13.5cm (5¼ inches)
13.5cm (5¼ inches)
15cm (6 inches)

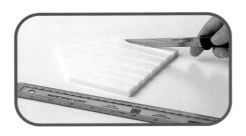

plank joins, indent with a knife and push the tip of a cocktail stick into the sugarpaste to make holes for the nails to slot in. Make a doorway template (see page 93) and position it against the front of the kennel. Cut the sugarpaste around it, and remove the piece. Thinly roll out 30g (1oz) white sugarpaste, cut out the door shape, using the template, and slot it into the gap. Measure one side of the roof. Roll out 140g (4½oz) white sugarpaste, marking lines as before. Cut a piece that is slightly larger than your measurements and stick in place. Cover the other side of the roof in the same way using another 140g (4½oz) paste. Roll out some of the trimmings and cut an oblong for the sign, marking the woodgrain and nail holes as before. Put aside to dry. Colour the remaining trimmings dark grey using black food colouring. Using half, roll a thin sausage and cut 25 tiny lengths for the nails, each no more than 5mm (¼ inch) long, and put aside to dry.

4 Before painting the cake, protect the cake board from splashes of colour by covering it completely with sheets of absorbent paper. Dilute a little black food colouring paste with water and paint the doorway black, using the firm bristle brush. Dilute some brown food colouring paste with water and paint the kennel, letting the colour run into the marked lines to highlight the woodgrain effect. Paint some brown on the underside and

edges of the roof. Add a little more water to the diluted brown, and paint a paler wash of colour over the door sign. Stick in position above the door.

ROOF

5 To make the blue painted roof effect, colour 125g (4oz) sugarpaste blue, then thinly roll out and cover the roof completely, trimming excess from around the edge. Smooth the blue sugarpaste unevenly around the roof edge to represent the paint runs. With the trimmings, model little flattened balls for the painted nail heads and stick along the top edge of the roof.

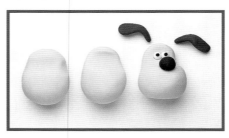

GROMIT

6 First colour 185g (6oz) sugarpaste cream, 22g (¾oz) brown and a small piece black. Using the photograph above as a guide and 155g (5oz) cream sugarpaste, model Gromit's head. Indent sockets for his eyes using the large end of a bone tool. Stick in position at the front of his kennel. Make two front paws using the remaining cream sugarpaste. Model teardrops and flatten slightly, then make a cut on each for the 'thumb', and two shorter cuts for the 'fingers'. Twist the thumbs and each finger to remove ridges and round off. Stick in position on either side of Gromit's head, resting on the cake board. For his ears, split the brown sugarpaste in half and model long,

slightly flattened teardrop shapes. Stick in position, bending each one round and securing against the kennel. Model two small balls of white sugarpaste for Gromit's eyes and stick them into the sockets. Using the black sugarpaste, model his nose and two pupils. Indent the centre of each pupil with the end of a paintbrush.

FINISHING

7 To make Gromit's bowl, colour 60g (2oz) sugarpaste green. Roll a ball and press down in the centre to indent. Shape the sides, pinching around the base to widen. Using sugar glue to secure, slot all the nails into the indented holes, then moisten the tip of each nail with a little sugar glue. Using the remaining dark grey sugarpaste, model tiny circles for the nail heads and press on to the nails. Draw Gromit's name on his bowl and on the door sign using the black food colouring pen. Pour the piping gel into the bowl for the water.

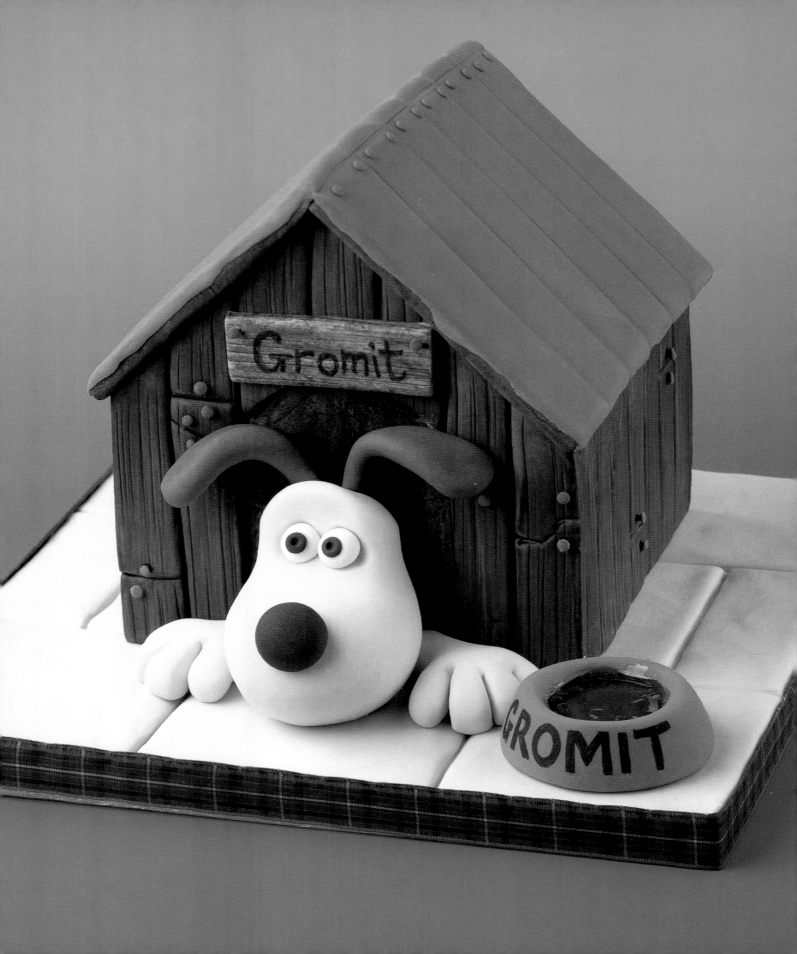

RUGRATS®

MATERIALS

25cm (10 inch) square cake (see page 12)
30cm (12 inch) round cake board
1.875kg (3¾lb) sugarpaste (rolled fondant)
440g (14oz) buttercream
625g (1¼lb) modelling paste
yellow, mauve, green, blue, orange, cream, brown, red, black and golden brown food colouring pastes
sugar glue
cool boiled water

☆

EQUIPMENT

large and small rolling pins
sharp knife
bone tool
fine paintbrush
pieces of foam
cocktail sticks (toothpicks)
medium star cutter

Tip
To make the chair arms more secure you can insert sugar sticks (see page 11) into the chair base, then lower the arms down on to them, sticking with sugar glue.

This cake is inspired by the brilliant world of the Rugrats from Nickelodeon. It's story-time and Tommy, the one-year-old hero, and his best friend Chuckie listen to tormenting cousin Angelica along with Spike, Chuckie's loyal dog, and an uninvited guest, the dreaded and terrifying Reptar!

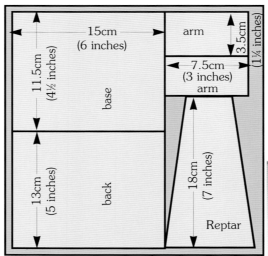

both arms until small and cylindrical, keeping the length. Shape the Reptar cake by trimming to round off ridges. Save all the cake trimmings. Sandwich the armchair layers together using buttercream, keeping the arms separate. Spread a thin layer of buttercream over the surface of the cake to help the sugarpaste stick.

1 Colour 375g (12oz) sugarpaste yellow. Roll out and cover the cake board. Trim the crust from the cake, slice the top flat and cut as shown in the diagram. Position the piece for the back of the chair on top of the base piece. Cut a 1cm (½ inch) deep layer from the Reptar cake and from this trim a seat cushion. Slice down on either side of the armchair from the top, cutting at a slight angle to shape the sides inwards. Trim

2 Colour 1kg (2lb) sugarpaste mauve. Roll out 875g (1¾lb) and cover the armchair, smoothing around the shape and pulling up a pleat at the back. Cut away, smooth the join closed, then trim excess from around the base. Position the armchair on the board. Using some

of the trimmings, model a rectangular piece for the front of the chair, to represent the bulging seat cushion, and stick in place with sugar glue. Spread a layer of buttercream on the front of the Reptar cake, then press against the back of the armchair. Using buttercream to stick cake trimmings together, build up Reptar's head on the top of the chair. Spread the remaining buttercream over the surface of the cake to help the sugarpaste stick.

smoothing downwards at the end. Use 22g (¾oz) green modelling paste to make the arms, curved eye sockets and nostrils. First model his two nostrils, indenting the centre of each with the small end of a bone tool, then make the two curved eye sockets and stick them in place with sugar glue. Using the photograph above as a guide, make the two arms. Roll a sausage, shaping a rounded end. Slightly flatten the rounded end and make two cuts for the fingers. Twist each finger to lengthen and remove ridges, and shape the ends to points. Repeat for the second arm. Stick in position using a little sugar glue. Colour 30g (1oz) modelling paste pale mauve. Using a little, model six claws, sticking each in place on the end of a finger, and make a tongue, indenting down the centre with the back of a knife. Stick the tongue on to Reptar's mouth, curling it upwards.

6 First colour 22g (¾oz) modelling paste mid-blue, 45g (1½oz) orange, 100g (3½oz) cream and 15g (½oz) yellow. Using the photograph, right, as a guide, make her legs from a little mid-blue paste by rolling thin sausage shapes tapering in at the ankle. Stick minute flattened dots of green modelling paste over the surface and carefully re-roll each leg to inlay the dots. Stick in position on the cake, leaving room for Chuckie, and bearing in mind that the chair arms have to go either side later.

Using 22g (¾oz) pale mauve modelling paste, roll two oval-shaped shoes, then model her dress, pinching around the base to flare out. Shape a little curved neckline by pinching up at the shoulders. Stick in position over the tights and to the back of the armchair, and stick her shoes in place. With a small amount of orange modelling paste, make Angelica's top by rolling a little ball to fill the neckline and two sausages for sleeves, flaring out at the ends. Press the end of a paintbrush into the sleeve ends to indent holes for the hands to slot in, and bend the right arm at the elbow.

Using 30g (1oz) cream modelling

REPTAR

3 Colour 500g (1lb) sugarpaste green. Using 155g (5oz), pad out Reptar's tail, smoothing against the cake until in line with the surface. Twist the end to a point. Roll out the remaining green and cover Reptar completely, tucking around his shape and carefully trimming excess without marking the armchair. Add a little sugar glue around Reptar's head, sticking the sugarpaste securely to the top of the armchair. Using the back of a knife, indent Reptar's wide mouth, extending it around the sides and twisting up the ends to give a wicked grin.

4 Colour 200g (6½oz) modelling paste green. Split 140g (4½oz) into two and model his legs and feet, shaping the toes with two cuts. Make each toe rounded,

CHAIR ARMS

5 Using the remaining mauve sugarpaste, roll out and cut strips to cover each chair arm. Position one arm cake down on to a strip, then wrap the sugarpaste around, smoothing the join closed. Repeat for the second arm. Place an arm upright on a piece of rolled-out sugarpaste and cut around. Use this to cover the end, again smoothing the join closed. Repeat for the opposite end, then cover the second arm in the same way. Press in at the front of each, model mauve buttons, and stick in place with sugar glue. Put aside to dry.

sticking them to the back of the arm-chair. Make two tiny bows from a small amount of pale mauve modelling paste.

CHUCKIE

7 First model Chuckie's teddy bear. Colour 7g (¼oz) modelling paste brown and use a small amount to model the teddy, using the end of a paintbrush to indent each ear. Knead some white into a small amount of brown to achieve a slightly paler colour and make the muzzle, tummy and foot pads. Make Chuckie's shorts using 15g (½oz) green modelling paste, pinching up at the top into a sit-ting position. Stick on to the chair, slight-ly twisted towards Angelica. Knead a small amount of white into some green to achieve a paler colour. Roll out and cut the tiny strips for his shorts.

With the remaining mid-blue model-ling paste, make Chuckie's top with two separate sleeves. Hollow out the base of the top to sit neatly on the shorts. Colour a small amount of modelling paste pink using a touch of red food colouring paste. Model the sleeve cuffs, indenting each in the centre to make a hole for the arms to slot in easily, and make a flat-tened ball for his collar, sticking every-thing in place with sugar glue as soon as it is made. Using 30g (1oz) cream model-ling paste, make two arms, cutting the hands as on page 11, and model two small pieces for Chuckie's knees. Make Chuckie's head, nose and ears. Indent a little at his mouth, using the end of a paintbrush, and shape a little chin. The nose is rounded with nostrils marked with the end of a cocktail stick. Stick all the pieces in position with the teddy in Chuckie's arms, again using some

paste, make Angelica's head, ears, nose and hands. For the hands, make tiny teardrop shapes and model as on page 11. Stick the points into the sleeve ends and bend the fingers of her left hand round. Make two tiny balls of paste for the ears, indenting the centre of each with the end of a paintbrush, and a tiny nose that is slightly pointed at the end. Model a ball for her head, indenting around the top to shape the eye area, keeping the bottom full and rounded. Make a cut for her open mouth with a knife, gently pulling the bottom lip down slightly. Stick the head in position against the back of the armchair, holding for a few moments to secure. Stick the nose and ears in place, then stick the sleeves and hands in position, sticking the raised hand against the side of her face. Use foam pieces for support whilst drying.

With 15g (½oz) white modelling paste, make two flattened balls for Angelica's eyes, and two flattened oval shapes for the soles of her shoes, mark-ing the heels with a knife, then roll out and cut three small oblongs for the book. Stick one oblong on top of another for the book's pages, indenting the centre to mark the fold. With the remaining oblong, mark twice in the centre to indent the binding, then stick the pages on top. Stick in position with Angelica's left hand holding the side.

With 7g (¼oz) yellow modelling paste, make the pieces for Angelica's hair as shown in the photograph above, the large flattened piece covering the top and back of her head. Build up the bunches,

foam pieces for support while drying.

Cut two small squares and tiny strips of mauve modelling paste for the frame of Chuckie's glasses. Colour 7g (¼oz) modelling paste black. Make a tiny flat-tened piece for Chuckie's open mouth, and model two minute pupils for his eyes. With yellow modelling paste, model the socks and a tiny flattened circle for the planet on his top. Colour a small amount of modelling paste red. Model Chuckie's shoes and roll a tiny piece for the planet ring. With white, make two soles for the shoes as before, cut two squares for his glasses, roll two laces and make his two front teeth. Stick his pupils and mouth in place.

With 22g (¾oz) orange modelling paste, make all the long, pointed teardrop shapes for Chuckie's hair, all in different lengths and curling at the ends. Stick one at a time over Chuckie's head, building up his spiky hair. For his freck-les, push the tip of a cocktail stick three times into each cheek. Stick the chair arms in position, using foam pieces to support the sides until dry.

TOMMY

8 To make Tommy, first model his nappy using 15g (½oz) white model-ling paste, hollowing out each leg hole with the large end of a bone tool. Using the remaining cream modelling paste, model Tommy's legs, arms, tummy, head, nose and ears. To make a leg, roll a sausage, then indent one end to shape an ankle and round off the top. Shape

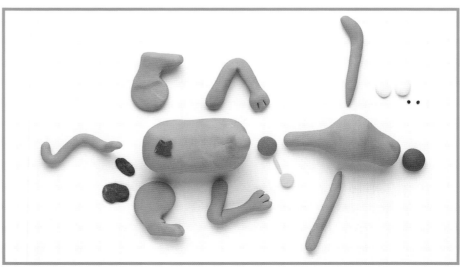

the top into a foot by pinching and bending down. Make tiny cuts for the toes, gently tapping to bend them around. Pinch up halfway along the length to shape a knee, indenting at the back to bend. For his tummy, model an oval shape, indenting the belly button with the tip of a cocktail stick. Shape his head, cutting his mouth open with a knife and pinching the top lip forwards. Make his ears as before and shape a little turned-up nose. Make a line of holes across the top of his head with the tip of a cocktail stick for the hair to slot in. Colour 30g (1oz) modelling paste pale blue. Using half, make his top and sleeves as before, smoothing up at the front so the tummy will show. Stick the pieces in position on the cake board, up against the bottom of the chair, with Tommy's head turned upwards towards Reptar. Model two yellow nappy pins, two slightly flattened white balls for his eyes, and two minute black pupils. For his hair, roll a very thin strand of black modelling paste and cut it into small lengths. Using a damp paintbrush to pick each one up, slot them into the holes on his head.

SPIKE

9 Colour 100g (3½oz) modelling paste golden brown. Using 45g (1½oz), model a fat sausage for Spike's body. Twist up one end to shape the bottom part of his neck, then indent around the centre for the dip in his back. Stick in position on the cake board with the bottom of his neck against the armchair. With a tiny piece of red modelling paste, make a flattened circle for his collar. To make his head, first roll a ball from 22g

(¾oz) paste, then shape his long, rounded muzzle. Twist a neck at the opposite end, pulling it downwards. Stick in position with the collar, supported on the seat of the armchair. With the remaining golden brown modelling paste, shape Spike's two long ears, front and back legs and a tail, sticking in place with sugar glue. With the remaining brown modelling paste, make his large ball nose. With a little white modelling paste, make his eyes. With some black, shape flattened pieces for his patches and two pupils for his eyes. Model a little yellow name tag for the dog collar. Stick everything in position with sugar glue.

FINISHING

10 To finish Reptar, model little triangular teeth from white modelling paste. Using 7g (¼oz) pale blue modelling paste, shape ten small half moons, graduating in size, for Reptar's scales. Cut twice on their rounded edges,

and smooth to remove ridges. Stick in a line down the centre of Reptar's back with the smaller scales at the front of his head and at the tip of his tail. With some orange, make Reptar's eyes, then model tiny strips for Angelica's socks, mark the ribbed pattern with a knife and stick around her ankles. Using a tiny amount of black, make Reptar's triangular pupils. To make the little ball, roll 7g (¼oz) green modelling paste into a ball, then thinly roll out and cut a mauve strip for the stripe. Thinly roll out orange and cut a star using the star cutter. Stick in position on the cake board. Roll thin sausages of pale blue modelling paste to trim around the chair arms and seat cushion. Model little flattened balls in varying sizes from the remaining coloured modelling pastes, and use to decorate the armchair. Dilute a little black food colouring paste with some water and, using a fine paintbrush, paint on Angelica's eyelashes and the print on the book cover.

RUPERT ™

One of the most popular cartoon characters ever created, Rupert Bear has been a firm favourite with generations of readers ever since he first appeared in the *Daily Express* 70 years ago.

Tip

Light confectioners' glaze is available in bottles from cake decorating suppliers. Pour some into a small bowl and brush over the sugarpaste to give the surface a shine.

BOARD

1 To decorate the cake board, first colour 410g (13oz) modelling paste pale blue, 90g (3oz) red, 45g (1½oz) orange, 100g (3½oz) yellow, 45g (1½oz) green and 45g (1½oz) mauve. Using 315g (10oz) pale blue, roll out and cover just over half of the cake board, trimming away excess. Cut a curve from one side to the other, remove the paste and reserve the trimmings. Using 45g (1½oz) each of red, orange, yellow, green, blue and mauve, roll out one at a time and cut tapering strips for the rainbow. Stick on to the cake board using sugar glue to secure. When the rainbow is complete, roll out the remaining pale blue and cover

the second half of the cake board. With the star cutter, cut out three stars at the end of the rainbow. Roll out 15g (½oz) yellow modelling paste, cut out three stars and slot into the spaces. Set the cake board aside to dry.

CAKES

2 Trim the crusts from both cakes. Using buttercream, sandwich the two cakes together, then spread a thin layer of buttercream over the surface of the cake to help the sugarpaste stick.

3 To make the cake balloon-shaped, pad the base with 250g (8oz) white sugarpaste, smoothing the ridge in line

with the cake surface. Shape the rounded end, pressing it down to rest on the work surface.

4 To cover the cake, colour 875g (1¾lb) sugarpaste blue. Roll out and cover the cake completely, pulling up a pleat. Cut the pleat away and smooth the join closed. Smooth the sugarpaste around the shape, tucking excess underneath. Lift carefully and position on the cake board, securing with a little sugar glue. For a completely smooth surface, polish with a cake smoother. Shape the balloon tie from blue sugarpaste trimmings and stick in place at the narrow end of the cake.

RUPERT

5 Put aside 7g (¼oz) yellow modelling paste for Rupert's scarf, then use the remaining yellow to make his trousers. Roll into a sausage, flatten slightly, then make a cut to separate the legs. Keeping the legs quite short, smooth to remove

ridges and twist down slightly. Pinch halfway along each leg to mark the knees and push in at the back to slightly bend and shape each knee. Stick the trousers on to the cake using sugar glue to secure.

To make Rupert's jumper, roll the remaining red modelling paste into a ball and flatten slightly. Make two cuts either side for the sleeves. Smooth to remove ridges and carefully twist each sleeve down to lengthen. Indent halfway along each sleeve and pinch out at the back to mark the elbows. Stick in position on the cake using foam pieces for support. Indent the end of each sleeve by pushing in the end of a paintbrush for the hands to slot in.

With the remaining yellow modelling paste, model an uneven circle of paste for Rupert's scarf, and roll out and cut the two scarf ends, frilling each by making small cuts with a knife. Stick in place. Push a sugar stick or piece of spaghetti down into the top of Rupert's body, leaving about half protruding.

To make Rupert's head, first roll 30g (1oz) white modelling paste into a ball, then shape a rounded muzzle. Press the circle cutter into the muzzle to mark Rupert's mouth, and indent a line using a knife. Press in the tip of a cocktail stick to open the mouth very slightly. Carefully lower Rupert's head on to the sugar stick, securing with sugar glue. Using 7g (¼oz) white, make his ears, indenting each with the end of the paintbrush, two teardrop-shaped shoes, two hands (see page 11) and his little oval-shaped nose, indenting the nostrils with the end of a paintbrush. Stick everything in place using sugar glue, supporting with foam pieces until dry.

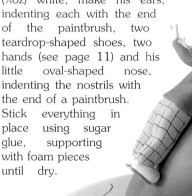

Colour a tiny amount of white modelling paste pale grey, using a touch of black food colouring and model two small shoe soles, marking the heels with a knife.

FINISHING

6 With the remaining white modelling paste, shape little clouds and place around the cake board. Leave the cake to dry, then paint a thin, even coat of light confectioners' glaze over the balloon. Draw in Rupert's eyes, the check pattern on his scarf and trousers, and the balloon string, using the black food colouring pen.

BABAR

Lovable Babar the elephant is ruler of Celesteville. The elephant elders were so impressed when they saw him in his shiny red convertible, they crowned him King!

™

MATERIALS

25cm (10 inch) square cake (see page 12)
30cm (12 inch) round cake board
1.25kg (2½lb) sugarpaste (rolled fondant)
315g (10oz) buttercream
625g (1¼lb) modelling paste
yellow, black, red and green food colouring pastes
sugar glue
sugar stick (see page 11) or length of raw dried spaghetti
light confectioner's glaze (see below)

☆

EQUIPMENT

large and small rolling pins
sharp knife
2.5cm (1 inch) circle cutter
miniature petal cutter
cocktail sticks (toothpicks)
no. 4 plain piping tube (tip) or miniature circle cutter
bone tool
medium paintbrush
black food colouring pen
ruler

Tip
Light confectioners' glaze is available in bottles from cake decorating suppliers. Pour some into a small bowl and brush over the sugarpaste to give the surface a shine.

Babar Characters ™ & © Laurent de Brunhoff.

BOARD & CAKE

1 Colour 375g (12oz) sugarpaste yellow, roll it out and use to cover the cake board. Put aside to dry. Trim the crusts from the cake and slice the top flat. Cut the cake exactly in half and put one piece on top of the other. Trim out a piece of cake for the seat area, making sure the front of the car is longer than the back. Cut around the edges from the top down to the second layer, trimming at an angle so the sides slope. To shape the tops of the doors, cut a curved piece out on each side. Starting at the back of the seat, trim the cake from the back of the car, rounding it off. Trim the front of the car to narrow it, then trim around the base of the car, cutting in at an angle.

2 Sandwich the two cake layers together using buttercream, then spread a thin layer of buttercream over the surface of the whole cake to help the sugarpaste stick. Position the cake on the cake board. Colour 125g (4oz) sugarpaste black. Thinly roll out just over half and cut a 2.5cm (1 inch) strip at least 50cm (20 inches) in length. Carefully roll up, position against the base of the cake, then unravel around the base, smoothing the join closed.

With the red sugarpaste trimmings, first model a tiny bow for Babar's tie and put aside, then roll two long thin sausages and stick either side of the car, joining them at each end to the points of the wheel bumpers. Colour 7g (¼oz) modelling paste black. To make the steering wheel, roll out and cut a circle using the 2.5cm (1 inch) circle cutter. Using the petal cutter, cut petal shapes out of the centre of the circle. Set aside to dry.

3 Colour 750g (1½lb) sugarpaste red. Roll out 625g (1¼lb) and cover the cake, smoothing around the shape and in and around the seat. Cut away the sugarpaste at the front, leaving the cake uncovered for the radiator grille. Trim excess sugarpaste from around the base in line with the top of the black strip. Thinly roll out the remaining black sugarpaste and cut out the seat back using the template on page 94. Mark lines with the back of a knife, radiating from the centre, then stick in place with a little sugar glue.

centre of each using the 2.5cm (1 inch) circle cutter, then stick in position on the cake using a little sugar glue to secure. Thinly roll out 30g (1oz) grey modelling paste, cut out the grille, using the template on page 94, and stick in place. With the grey trimmings, roll four small balls for the centres of the wheels and make the emblem for the top of the radiator. Split 125g (4oz) red sugarpaste into four equal pieces and shape four teardrop-shaped wheel bumpers. Stick in position over the wheels and against the car sides.

BABAR

5 First model a rounded teardrop for Babar's body using 125g (4oz) white modelling paste. Colour 60g (2oz) modelling paste green. Using half, thinly roll out and cut Babar's waistcoat, jacket and collar using the templates on page 94. Mark a join down the centre of the waist-

WHEELS, GRILLE, BUMPERS, ETC.

4 To make the wheels, first colour 410g (13oz) modelling paste grey using a touch of black colouring paste. Split 250g (8oz) into four equal pieces. Roll each piece into a ball and flatten slightly. Mark the

coat using the back of a knife, then stick in position with a little sugar glue. Stick the jacket on next, wrapping it around Babar's body and smoothing it around to the front. Attach the collar and carefully position Babar's body in the car. Stick his bow tie in place. Split the remaining green modelling paste in half and make the two sleeves, marking creases halfway along using a cocktail stick. Slightly flatten the sleeves at the shoulder, pinch at the back of the elbow to shape and bend, then stick in position. Model two flattened circles of white modelling paste for the end of each sleeve and stick in place.

at the top outer edges. Indent two holes for the tusks using the bone tool. To help hold Babar's head in place, moisten a sugar stick or piece of spaghetti with sugar glue and insert it into Babar's body, leaving about 2.5cm (1 inch) protruding. Carefully lower his head down on to the sugar stick, and secure in place. Model two tusks from white modelling paste and insert into the holes. Stick the steering wheel in position. Colour the remaining modelling paste yellow. Roll out and cut out Babar's crown using the template on page 94. Stick the two ends together to make the crown circular, then position on top of Babar's head. Leave the cake to dry for at least 8 hours, or overnight.

FINISHING

7 To give the car a shine, paint 2–3 thin coats of light confectioners' glaze over the car, seat and bumpers, leaving each coat to dry thoroughly before applying the next. Using the black food colouring pen, draw in Babar's waistcoat buttons and eyes, then add an edging line around the grille, and a criss-cross pattern over the grille, using a ruler if necessary.

6 Using the remaining grey, model two flattened circles for Babar's front feet and mark nails using the no. 4 plain piping tube. Stick in position on the sleeve ends. To make Babar's head, roll a ball, then twist up a trunk and slightly indent the end with a bone tool. Pinch the paste out on either side of his head to shape the ears, pinching each thinner

CTW

SESAME STREET®

Let Big Bird, Elmo and Ernie, three of the famous and ever-popular characters from Sesame Street, burst out in style at your child's party.

MATERIALS

30x20cm (12x8 inch) oblong cake (see page 12)
30cm (12 inch) hexagonal cake board
1.5kg (3lb) sugarpaste (rolled fondant)
410g (13oz) buttercream
675g (1lb 6oz) modelling paste
60g (2oz) royal icing
blue, yellow, green, red, pink, black, orange and navy food colouring pastes
sugar glue
3 stamens for feathers (see below)

EQUIPMENT

large and small rolling pins
sharp knife
foam sheet
medium and large star cutters
3 piping bags
pieces of foam
cocktail stick (toothpick)

Tip

The stamens used as feathers in the top of Big Bird's head must be removed before the cake is served.

(diagram: 30cm (12 inches) wide × 20 cm (8 inches) tall, divided into six squares labelled 1, 2, 3 on the top row and 1, 2, 3 on the bottom row)

BOARD & CAKE

1 Colour 500g (1lb) sugarpaste blue. Roll out and cover the cake board, then put aside to dry. Trim the crusts from the cake, slice the top flat and cut as in the diagram. Put one cake square on top of another to make a cube and, if necessary, re-trim to make sure the sides are straight. Repeat for the other squares so you have three cube-shaped cakes.

CUBES

2 Sandwich the layers in each cube together using buttercream, then spread a thin layer of buttercream over

the surfaces of all the cubes to help the sugarpaste stick. Roll out white sugarpaste, a little at a time, place one side of one cube down on to it and cut around. Repeat until all the sides are covered, then cover the remaining two cubes in the same way. To help the base of the 'A' cube hold its shape when positioned on top of the other cubes, place on a foam sheet to dry. Using 30g (1oz) white modelling paste, thinly roll out and cut a square to fit the top of a cube. Position on the top, securing with sugar glue around the edge only. Cut a small cross, then a plus sign over it, directly into this top layer, slightly to the left, and pull up the small points to give a 'bursting' effect. Repeat for the remaining two cakes, using 30g (1oz) modelling paste for each. Position the 'burst' on the 'C' cube slightly towards the right, and a larger 'burst' centrally on the 'A' cube.

3 Put the 'B' cube on the cake board, turning it slightly outwards. Colour 250g (8oz) modelling paste yellow, 75g (2½oz) green and 170g (5½oz) red. Using 75g (2½oz) yellow, thinly roll out and cut out strips to edge the 'B' cube. Thinly roll out the trimmings and cut out two stars using the large star cutter. Stick in

ELMO

5 Split 30g (1oz) red modelling paste in half. Model Elmo's oval head using one piece, then split the other piece into three equally sized pieces. Make his body with one, and then his two arms. To make an arm, roll a sausage of paste, pinching near the end to shape a wrist. Pinch all the way around to round off the end, then flatten the end slightly. Make a cut for the thumb, then two slightly shallower cuts for the fingers. Pinch to shape rounded fingers. Roll out some of the remaining black, and cut out Elmo's smile. Model two flattened black balls for his pupils. Using white, roll two balls for his eyes. Colour 45g (1½oz) modelling paste orange. Roll a small piece into a ball for

position on two sides of the cube. Using the 'B' template (see page 93), cut out two letters and stick in position on the front and back with sugar glue. Repeat for the 'C' cube, using all of the green, then for the 'A' cube, using 75g (2½oz) red. Using sugar glue to secure, assemble the cakes on the board, making sure the gap between the two bottom cakes is small enough to give sufficient support to the top 'A' cube. To decorate the cake board edge, thinly roll out 45g (1½oz) red modelling paste and cut a long, thin strip. Stick it around the cake board edge, creating a wavy effect. With the medium star cutter, cut away part of the red strip at each corner. Thinly roll out 15g (½oz) yellow modelling paste and cut stars to fill the spaces, securing with sugar glue.

red trimmings, shape a tongue. Roll two white balls for his eyes. Colour a minute amount of modelling paste pink, some more blue and a little more black. Make Big Bird's eyelids using the pink, roll out and cut tiny blue strips, then model two tiny flattened black balls for the pupils. Stick everything in position with sugar glue, then stick Big Bird in place on top of the cake. Colour 45g (1½oz) royal icing yellow and put in a piping bag. Cut a small hole in the tip and pipe teardrop-shaped balls of yellow royal icing all over Big Bird for his feathers.

BIG BIRD

4 To make Big Bird, model a teardrop-shaped body using 45g (1½oz) yellow modelling paste, then cut the bottom straight. With 75g (2½oz), roll a ball for the head, pressing the front slightly flat for the face. Using the trimmings, model a small bottom beak, shaping a rounded end, and a larger top beak that is a little more pointed at the end. Stick the large beak on the centre of Big Bird's face with the small beak directly underneath it. Stick a minute amount of yellow paste on the end of each of the three stamens, using sugar glue, then insert the ends into the top of Big Bird's head. Using some of the

Elmo's nose. Assemble Elmo on the 'B' cube with his arms up. If necessary, support his pose with pieces of foam whilst drying. Colour 7g (¼oz) royal icing red and put in a piping bag. Snip a small hole in the tip and pipe Elmo's fur, dragging the bag over the surface so only a little icing comes out, and making sure the sugarpaste beneath is still visible.

ERNIE

6 Split 30g (1oz) yellow modelling paste in half. With one piece, model Ernie's body. With the other piece, make two sleeves, a flattened circle for his collar and two slightly smaller flattened circles for the cuffs at the end of each sleeve. Indent around the edge of all three flattened circles with the tip of a cocktail stick to mark a rib effect. Colour 7g (¼oz) modelling paste navy blue. Thinly roll out 7g (¼oz) red and all the navy and cut thin strips. Stick alternate colours over his body and sleeves. Stick Ernie's body and sleeves in position (with the collar and cuffs), 'bursting' out of the 'C' cube. Using 30g (1oz) orange modelling paste, make Ernie's oval head. Cut a smile just below the centre, then smooth with your finger to open the mouth. With the remaining orange modelling paste, make two hands (as before) and two ears. With the remaining red, roll a ball for his nose and thinly roll out and cut a smile, inserting it carefully into his mouth and securing with sugar glue. With white modelling paste, make two eyes, and model two black pupils. Colour the

remaining royal icing black and put in a piping bag. Cut a small hole in the tip and pipe Ernie's spiky hair by squeezing the black royal icing out on to the top of his head, then pulling gently upwards to create points.

Tip

The alphabet cubes are covered in white sugarpaste to cut down on the amount of food colouring used.

Every pre-school child's best friend, Barney™ the world-famous dinosaur helps children discover the joys of learning, imagination, make-believe and love.

MATERIALS

25x20cm (10x8 inch) oblong cake
(see page 12)
30cm (12 inch) square cake board
1.25kg (2½lb) sugarpaste (rolled fondant)
685g (1lb 6oz) modelling paste
200g (6½oz) buttercream
mauve, orange, pink, green, purple, yellow, black, red and blue food colouring pastes
sugar glue
3 sugar sticks (see page 11) or lengths of raw dried spaghetti

☆

EQUIPMENT

large and small rolling pins
sharp knife
ruler
fine paintbrush
cocktail sticks (toothpicks)
bone tool
small circle cutter
pieces of foam

BOARD & CAKE

1 Colour 440g (14oz) sugarpaste mauve, roll out and cover the cake board, then put aside to dry. Cut the crusts from the cake, keeping the top rounded where it has risen. Trim a wedge from the centre to represent the middle of the book, then trim to slope the pages down towards the centre. Trim the ends of the cake, cutting down at an inward angle. Spread a coat of buttercream over the surface of the cake to help the sugarpaste stick, then position the cake at an angle on the cake board.

BOOK

2 Roll out 315g (10oz) white sugarpaste and cut strips to cover the sides of the cake. Use your fingers to indent at the back and front of the cake to mark the centre of the page binding. Using a knife, mark all the page lines.

3 Measure the top of the cake with a ruler. Roll out 250g (8oz) white sugarpaste, cut out an oblong to fit the top of the book, and lay it in place. Roll out the

remaining white sugarpaste, cut an oblong as before and position it on the book for the top pages. Using the shape templates on page 94, position them on the cake and cut around them, cutting down through the top layer of sugar-paste only. Remove each cut-out shape and reserve the trimmings.

4 To make the book binding, colour 45g (1½oz) modelling paste orange. Roll it out thinly, cut strips, and stick them against the cake sides, smoothing the joins closed. Press the end of a paint-brush into the back and front of the cake to mark folds in the cover at the top and bottom of the book 'spine'. Colour 15g (½oz) modelling paste pale pink, 15g (½oz) mauve and 30g (1oz) green. Using all of the pink and mauve, and half of the green, thinly roll out and cut a pink heart, a mauve hexagon and a green oval, again using the templates. Slot them into the spaces on the page. Using the mauve modelling paste trimmings, press small teardrop-shaped pieces into the hollows at the back and front of the cake where the pages join.

BARNEY™

5 First colour 425g (13½oz) modelling paste purple, 45g (1½oz) yellow and 7g (¼oz) black. For Barney's body, model a teardrop shape using 250g (8oz) pur-ple modelling paste, twisting up a tail at the back. To make his legs, split 75g (2½oz) in half and roll two fat sausages. Twist to shape an ankle and round off the end of each leg, then pinch out the

feet. Make cuts for the toes and pinch around the top of each toe to round off. Position Barney's body and legs on top of the cake, securing with sugar glue. To help support the head and arms, push sugar sticks down into the body, brushing each first with a little sugar glue.

For Barney's head, roll a ball using 75g (2½oz) purple paste, shaping a rounded muzzle at the front. Smooth underneath the muzzle to indent Barney's mouth area and shape the top of his head by pinching either side. Mark nostrils with the tip of a cocktail stick and indent eye sockets with a bone tool. Using sugar glue to secure, carefully lower Barney's head down on to the sugar stick until in position.

Put aside a minute amount of purple modelling paste for Barney's eyelids, then split the remaining piece in half and roll two sausages for his arms. Twist the wrists and round off the ends for the hands, then flatten slightly. Make small cuts for the thumbs and smooth to round off. Push the arms down on to the sugar sticks, thumbs upwards, securing with sugar glue.

Roll out a tiny amount of black mod-elling paste and shape a tiny half moon for Barney's smile, then model two pupils for his eyes. Using a tiny amount of white modelling paste, roll two balls for his eyes and two tiny highlights. Stick

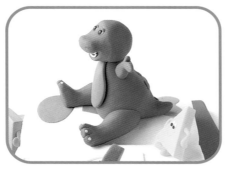

in place in the eye sockets with the pupils and highlights. Make two tiny strips of white modelling paste for Barney's teeth, each tapering to a point at either end, and stick in position with the black 'smile'. With the tiny piece of reserved purple modelling paste, model two tiny eyelids and stick in position with sugar glue. Roll six tiny balls of yellow modelling paste, flatten, then stick one on to each toe. To finish Barney, use the remaining green modelling paste to make his rounded teardrop-shaped tummy, then model four different-sized flattened balls and stick over his back and tail.

CHARACTER SHAPES

6 Colour 45g (1½oz) modelling paste red and 45g (1½oz) blue. Thickly roll out the red, and use the circle template to cut out a circle. Indent the eye sockets with a bone tool and mark the smile just underneath with the small circle cutter. To dimple the smile, push the end of a paintbrush into each corner. Using the red trimmings, make two teardrop-shaped feet and two arms with rounded hands. Assemble on the cake using

pieces of foam for support whilst drying. Using white, make two tiny teardrop-shaped eyes and model two black pupils. Stick the eyes in place with the pointed ends upwards. Using the blue and yellow modelling paste, make the square and tri-angular characters in the same way.

Templates

FIREMAN SAM™
(pages 14–18)
Bonnet

FIREMAN SAM™
(pages 14–18)
Side window

FIREMAN SAM™
(pages 14–18)
Windscreen

THE WOMBLES™
(pages 24–27)
Flag logo

DENNIS & GNASHER™
(pages 32–35)
Dennis's eyes

MY LITTLE PONY
(pages 28–31)
Front door

BANANAS IN PYJAMAS™
(pages 56–59)
Collar

Shoe bands

BANANAS IN PYJAMAS™
(pages 56–59)
Shoe soles

THE FLOWER FAIRIES™
(pages 19–23)

Black Medick Boy
Fairy's headscarf

Black Medick Boy
Fairy's wings

Horse Chestnut
Fairy wings

Black Medick Girl
Fairy's wings

Black Medick leaf

Bindweed
calyx

Bindweed
Fairy's wings

Bindweed
Fairy's hat leaf

Black Medick Girl
Fairy's dress leaf

Mulberry Fairy
wings

Bindweed leaf

Candytuft
Fairy wings

Candytuft leaf

Mulberry leaves

Mulberry
Fairy's
waistcoat

SUPER MARIO™
(pages 60–63)
Hat badge

SUPER MARIO™
(pages 60–63)
Shoe soles

SUPER MARIO™
(pages 60–63)
Hat wing

SUPER MARIO™
(pages 60–63)
Moustache

SUPER MARIO™ (pages 60–63)
Hat peak (visor)

WALLACE & GROMIT™
(pages 69–71)
Kennel doorway

SUPER MARIO™
(pages 60–63) Eyes & eyebrows

SUPER MARIO™
(pages 60–63)
Braces

SESAME STREET™
(pages 84–87)
Letters

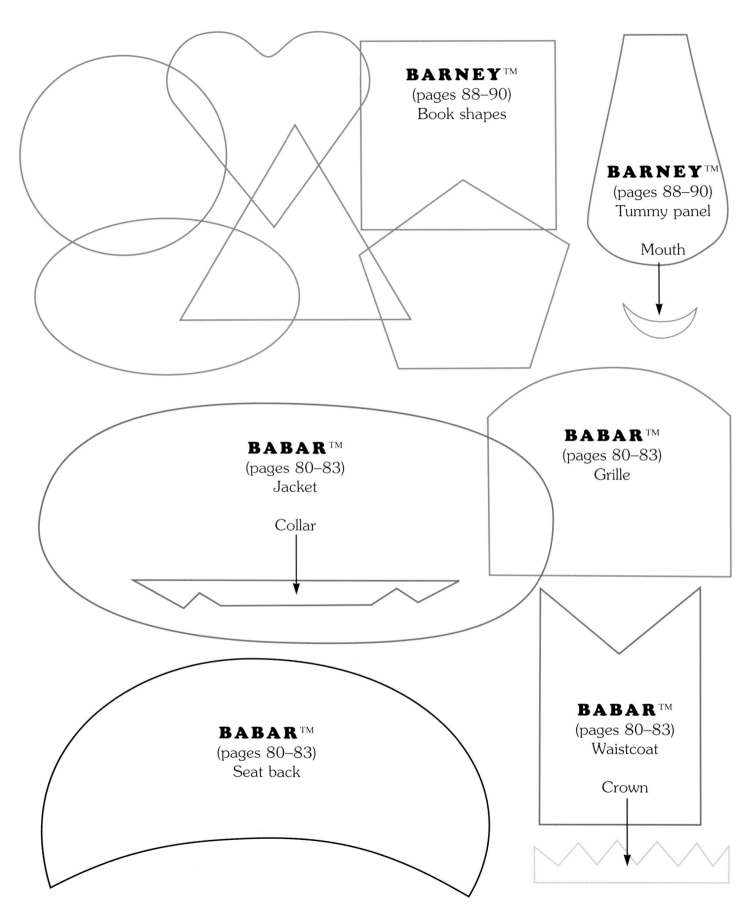

BARNEY™
(pages 88–90)
Book shapes

BARNEY™
(pages 88–90)
Tummy panel

Mouth

BABAR™
(pages 80–83)
Jacket

Collar

BABAR™
(pages 80–83)
Grille

BABAR™
(pages 80–83)
Waistcoat

BABAR™
(pages 80–83)
Seat back

Crown

Index

ACKNOWLEDGEMENTS

The author would like to thank the following:

Barbara Croxford, for always being so enthusiastic, helpful and totally professional.
Clive Streeter for wonderful photography, and always being so patient.

My nephews, David and Craig Brown, for laughing at the mess I get in and pinching cake crumbs.
My children, Lewis, Laura and Shaun, who helped with all the designs and ran endless errands.
Paul, my husband, for making sure I'm never late.
Doris and George, for being there when needed. I am so grateful.

The author and publishers would also like to thank the following suppliers:

Cake Art Ltd.
Venture Way,
Crown Estate,
Priorswood, Taunton,
Devon TA2 8DE

Guy, Paul and Co. Ltd.
Unit B4, Foundry Way,
Little End Road,
Eaton Socon,
Cambs. PE19 3JH

Renshaw Scott Ltd.
Crown Street,
Liverpool L8 7RF

Other distributors and retailers

Squires Kitchen
Squires House,
3 Waverley Lane,
Farnham,
Surrey GU9 8BB
Tel: 01252 711749

Confectionery Supplies
31 Lower Cathedral Road,
Riverside,
Cardiff,
S. Glamorgan,
CF1 8LU
Tel: 01222 372161

Cakes & Co.
25 Rock Hill,
Blackrock Village,
Co. Dublin,
Ireland
Tel: (01) 283 6544

Beryl's Cake Decorating & Pastry Supplies
P.O. Box 1584, N.
Springfield, VA22151-0584 USA
Tel: 1-800-488-2749
Fax: 703-750-3779

Cake Decorators' Supplies
Shop 1,
770 George Street,
Sydney 2001
Australia
Tel: 61 02 92124050

Also available by Debbie Brown, the hugely popular *Favourite Character Cakes*. Filled with a host of different cake designs, this fabulous book provides many more favourite characters to choose from.

Includes:
THOMAS THE TANK ENGINE
BUDGIE THE LITTLE HELICOPTER™
PEANUTS™
SPOT
SOOTY™
POPEYE™
PADDINGTON BEAR™
POSTMAN PAT™
PETER RABBIT & FRIENDS™
FOREVER FRIENDS™
OLD BEAR™
NODDY™
WHERE'S WALLY™
THE SMURFS™
MR MEN™
BETTY BOOP™
WIND IN THE WILLOWS
COUNTRY COMPANIONS™

ISBN 1-85391-656-0

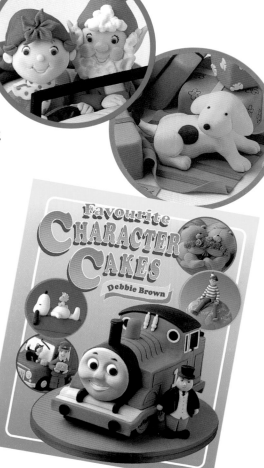